*A spectre is haunting
our universities—
the spectre of a
radical and militant
nationally co-ordinated
movement for*
student power.

—Carl Davidson,
The New Radicals in the Multiversity
(1967)

CHARLES H. KERR SIXTIES SERIES

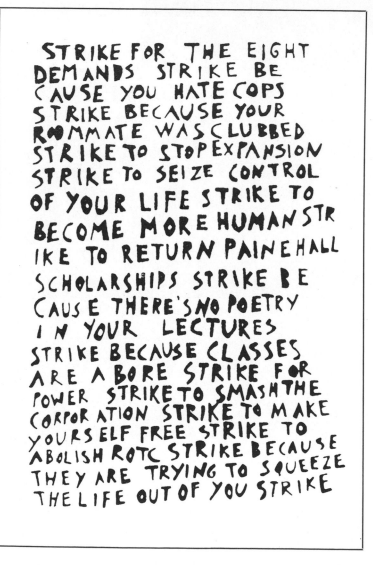

Harvard University Student Strike Poster (Spring 1969)

CARL DAVIDSON

THE NEW RADICALS
IN THE MULTIVERSITY
and other SDS writings on
STUDENT SYNDICALISM

(1966-67)

*with a new Afterword
by the Author*

Sixties Series
Number Two

CHICAGO
Charles H. Kerr Publishing Company
1990

About the Author

Carl Davidson was born in 1943 and grew up in Aliquippa, Pennsylvania, a small Ohio river valley mill town. The first of his family to go to college, he took part in the student peace and civil rights battles of the early 1960s, including a long freedom march through Mississippi. After a year as a roving organizer in the Great Plains, he served as national vice-president and inter-organizational secretary of Students for a Democratic Society (SDS) in 1966-68. Later he became a staff writer and editor of *The Guardian*, and a national leader of the antiwar movement. Today he is managing editor of *Insight Features*, an alternative news service for progressive media.

The photograph reproduced on the cover was taken during the student strike at Columbia University, New York, 1968.

Printed on recycled paper.

ISBN 0-88286-177-8 *paper*
0-88286-178-6 *cloth*

594

Send for our complete catalog.
Charles H. Kerr Publishing Company
Established 1886
P. O. Box 914, Chicago, Illinois 60690

THE NEW RADICALS
IN THE MULTIVERSITY

The student movement has come under criticism from both the right and the left for its lack of a coherent ideology and strategy for social change. While there is certainly a great deal of truth in this criticism, my sensibilities tell me that this lack may be more to our advantage than to our disadvantage. To my mind, the great strength of the New Left has been its unconscious adherence to Marx's favorite motto—doubt everything. The student movement is young and inexperienced; yet, it has shown great wisdom in maintaining the principle that political truth must come from political experience. Ideology is not something sucked out of thumbs, nor found in this or that set of political catechisms. Rather, political analysis and strategy is something that grows slowly out of years of political experience and struggle. It must find its beginnings and maintain its deepest roots in people's day-to-day life-activity, for it is social reality that we are trying to understand and change.

In deepening that understanding of social reality, we must always remember that "The dispute over the reality or non-reality of thinking that is isolated from practice is a purely *scholastic* question."[1] Too often we are bogged down in theoretical disputes when the only way we can answer those questions is in *practice*, in political experimentation, in action. This is why we must remain open on many political questions. But this is not to say that we should only "do what the spirit say do." The concept of practical-critical activity (*i.e.*, praxis) is three-sided: we must *act*, then *reflect* on the activity, and finally *criticize* the activity. The progress of action, reflection, and criticism must be repeated again and again. The body of knowledge, ever changing and expanding, that grows from this process emerges as an ideology. Finally, the process is historical; it develops over a period of time.

It is for these reasons, as well as the fact that we are young and politically inexperienced, that we must emphasize an ongoing *practical-critical activity* over and above any allegiance to theoretical certitude. I hope that my following remarks on theory, strategy, and tactics will be taken in this context. All my assertions come from a limited experience and, as such, are open to criticism, revision, and the acid-test of political practice.

Part One
THE PRESENT MALAISE OF EDUCATION

"Happiness Is Student Power" was the most catching slogan emblazoned on the many banners and picket signs during the Berkeley Student Strike in December, 1966. But, as most college administrators know only too well, Berkeley and its rebellious student body is not an isolated phenomenon among the vast variety of American campuses. Far from being an exception, Berkeley has become the paradigm case of the educational malaise in the United States; and, in the last few years, that malaise has been transformed into a movement. Indeed, a spectre is haunting our universities—the spectre of a radical and militant nationally co-ordinated movement for *student power.*

Students began using the slogan "student power" soon after black people in the civil rights movement made the demand for "black power." Are students niggers?* After studying the history of the Wobblies and labor syndicalism, students started thinking about student syndicalism. Are students workers? Power for what? Just any old kind of power? The university is a clumsy and un-coordinated machine, engulfing and serving thousands of people. Do students want to be administrators?

Obviously the cry for "power" in and of itself is a vacuous demand. Student power is not so much something we are fighting *for*, as it is something we must have in order to gain specific objectives. Then what are the objectives? What is our program? There is much variety and dispute on these questions. But there is one thing that seems clear. However the specific forms of our immediate demands and programs may vary, the long-range goal and the daily drive that motivates and directs us is our intense longing for our liberation. In short, what the student power movement is about is *freedom.*

But aren't students free? Isn't America a democracy, even if it is a little manipulative? To answer those kinds of questions and many others that are more serious, it is important to look more

---

* "Student as Nigger" was the title of a much-reprinted article by Prof. Jerry Farber of California State University at Los Angeles. It likened administration/faculty discrimination against students to the U.S. system of institutionalized racism against African-Americans (Publisher's Note).

6

closely and come to an understanding of the malaise motivating our movement.

What do American students think of the educational institutions in which they live an important part of their lives? The most significant fact is that most of them don't think about them. Such young men and women made up that apathetic majority we called the "silent generation" in the 1950s. While the last few years has shown a marked and dramatic growth of a new radicalism, we should not forget that the apathetic and the cynical among the student population are still in the majority. But this need not be discouraging. In fact, we should view that apparent apathy among the majority of students with a certain qualified optimism.

What makes people apathetic? My feeling is that apathy is the *unconscious* recognition students make of the fact that they are *powerless*. Despite all the machinations and rhetoric used by hot-shot student politicos within administration-sponsored student governments, people's experience tells them that nothing changes. Furthermore, if and when change does occur, students fully recognize that they were powerless to effect those changes in one way or another. If this is in fact the case, then why shouldn't students be apathetic? The administration rules, despite the facade of student governments, of dorm councils, and of student judicials. And when *they* give us ex-officio seats on *their* academic committees, the result among most students is that deeper, more hardened kind of apathy—cynicism.

The apathetic students are correct *as far as they go*. They are powerless. The forms given us for our self-government are of the Mickey Mouse, sand-box variety. I would only be pessimistic if a majority of students really accepted the illusion that those institutions had meaning in their lives, or that they could significantly affect those institutions. But the opposite is the case. The apathy reflects the *reality* of their powerlessness. When that reality confronts the lie of the official rhetoric, the contradiction is driven home—and the apathetic become the cynical. What that contradiction—that daily living with a lie—all adds up to is a *dynamic* tension and alienation. And that, fellow organizers, is the necessary subjective condition for any revolution.

It is important to understand that students are alienated from much more than the social and extracurricular aspect of their education. In fact, their deepest alienation is directed at the educa-

7

tion process itself. The excerpts that follow are from a letter written to the *New York Times* by a young woman student:

"I came to this school not thinking I could even keep up with the work. I was wrong. I can keep up. I can even come out on top. My daily schedule's rough. I get up at 6:30. . . After dinner I work until midnight or 12:30. In the beginning, the first few weeks or so, I'm fine. Then I begin to wonder just what this is all about: am I educating myself? I have that one answered. . . I'm educating myself the way *they* want. So I convince myself the real reason I'm doing all this is to prepare myself; meantime I'm wasting those years of preparation. I'm not learning what I want to learn. . . I don't care about the feudal system. I want to know about life. I want to think and read. When?. . . My life is a whirlpool. I'm caught up in it, but I'm not conscious of it. I'm what *you* call living, but somehow I can't find life. . . So maybe I got an A. . . but when I get it back I find that A means nothing. It's a letter *you* use to keep me going. . . I wonder what I'm doing here. I feel phony; I don't belong. . . You wonder about juvenile delinquents. If I ever become one, I'll tell why it will be so. I feel cramped. I feel like I'm in a coffin and can't move or breathe. . . My life is worth nothing. It's enclosed in a few buildings on one campus; it goes no further. I've got to bust."[2]

Tell the truth. Every American student knows that's the way it is. Even our administrators recognize what is going on. In 1963, a year or so *before* the first Berkeley insurrection, Clark Kerr* prophesized, "the undergraduate students are restless. Recent changes in the American university have done them little good. . . There is an incipient revolt. . ."[3] Kerr is not only concerned about the students. He also casts a worried glance at the faculty. "Knowledge is now in so many bits and pieces and administration so distant that faculty members are increasingly members in a 'lonely crowd,' intellectually and institutionally."[4] The academic division of labor and depersonalization among the faculty is more than apparent to the students. Incoming freshmen scratch their heads, trying to understand *any* possible relevance

---

* Liberal educator Clark Kerr (no relation to Charles H. Kerr!) was President of the University of California during the 1960s. In numerous books and articles he set forth his view that the American university (or "multiversity") was essentially a "knowledge factory," and that its principal function was to serve the needs of industry, government and the military (Publisher's Note).

of many of the courses in the catalogue, some of which they are required to take. Also, some of the best belly-laughs are had by reading the titles of master's and doctoral theses, like one granted a Ph.Ed. at Michigan State University: "An Evaluation of Thirteen Brands of Football Helmets on the Basis of Certain Impact Measures."[5] What's worse, even if a course seems as though it might be relevant to our lives, like Psychology or Political Science, we are soon told by our prof that what we'll learn only has to do with the laboratory behavior of rats, and that "political science" has nothing to do with day-to-day politics. A student from Brandeis sums it up nicely, "By the time we graduate, we have been painstakingly trained in separating facts from their meaning. . . . No wonder that our classes, with few exceptions, seem irrelevant to our lives. No wonder they're so boring. Boredom is the necessary condition of any education which teaches us to manipulate the facts and suppress their meaning."[6] Irrelevancy, meaninglessness, boredom, and fragmentation are the kinds of attributes that are becoming more and more applicable to mass education in America. We are becoming a people required to know more and more about less and less. This is true not only for our students, but also for our teachers; not only in our universities, but also in our secondary and primary schools—private as well as public.

What should education be about in America? The official rhetoric seems to offer an answer: education should be the process of developing the free, autonomous, creative and responsible *individual*—the "citizen," in the best sense of the word. Furthermore, higher education ought to encourage and enable the individual to turn his personal concerns into social issues, open to rational consideration and solution. C. Wright Mills put it clearly: "The aim of the college, for the individual student, is to eliminate the need in his life for the college; the task is to help him become a self-educating man. For only that will set him free."[7]

But what is the reality of American education? Contrary to our commitment to individualism, we find that the day-to-day practice of our schools is authoritarian, conformist, and almost entirely status oriented. We find the usual relationship between teacher and student to be a disciplined form of dominance and subordination. We are told of the egalitarianism inherent in our

9

school system, where the classroom becomes the melting-pot for the classless society of America's "people's capitalism," where everyone has the opportunity to climb to the top. Again, the opposite is the case. Our schools are more racially segregated now (1967) than ever before. There is a clear class bias contained both within and among our public schools—not even considering the clear class nature of our private schools and colleges. Within the secondary schools, students are quickly channeled—usually according to the class background of their parents—into vocational, commercial, or academic preparatory programs. Concerning the class differences among our public schools, James Conant remarks in *Slums and Suburbs*, "one cannot imagine the possibility of a wealthy suburban district deliberately consolidating with other districts to achieve a truly comprehensive high school in which students of all abilities and socio-economic backgrounds will study together."[8] Even if they did consolidate, the problem would only be rationalized, rather than solved. Who knows? Maybe the class struggle would break out on the playground.

Finally, what about that traditional American ideal that we were all taught to honor—the legend of the self-educated and self-educating man? It seems to me that rather than enabling an individual to initiate and engage himself in a continual and coherent lifelong educational process, our public programs are the sort where an individual is merely subjected to a random series of isolated training situations.

From individual freedom to national service, from egalitarianism to class and racial hierarchical ossification, from self-reliance to institutional dependence—we have come to see education as the mechanistic process of homogeneous, uncritical absorption of "data" and development of job skills. But it is something more than that. The socialization and acculturation that goes on within American educational institutions is becoming increasingly central in the attempts to mold and shape American youth. This is mainly the result of the declining influence and, in some cases, the collapse of other traditional socializing institutions such as the church and the family. The schools, at all levels, end up with the job of maintaining, modifying, and transmitting the dominant themes of the national culture.

Quantitatively education has been rapidly increasing in the last few decades; but, as it grows in size, it decreases *qualitatively*.

Rickover states in *Education and Freedom*: "We end up where we began a hundred years ago—with an elementary vocational education for the majority, and a poor college preparatory course for a minority of students."[9] Conant, who is quite concerned with the plight of the 80-85% of urban non-college bound high school students who are "social dynamite," places as a primary goal of education, giving these students "the kind of zeal and dedication. . . to withstand the relentless pressures of communism."[10]

What about our school teachers? How is the nation faring on that front? Over 30% of the students in U.S. colleges and universities are going into primary and secondary education. However, despite the quantity, Mortimer Smith remarks in *The Diminished Mind*, "the teacher-training institutions. . . are providing us with teachers who are our most poorly educated citizens."[11] While the job of teacher should command the highest respect in any society, many of us are well aware of the fact that in relation to other parts of the university, the college or school of education is considered to be the intellectual slum of the campus.

It seems clear that bourgeois education in the U.S. is in its historically most irrational and decadent state. Primary, secondary, and the university systems are fusing together, thoroughly rationalizing and dehumanizing their internal order, and placing themselves in the service of the state, industry, and the military. Kerr is quite clear about this when he speaks of the "multiversity" making a common-law marriage with the federal government. John Hannah, president of Michigan State, was even more clear in a speech given in September, 1961: "Our colleges and universities must be regarded as bastions of our defense, as essential to the preservation of our country and way of life as super-sonic bombers, nuclear powered submarines and intercontinental ballistics missiles."[12] The fact that none of these three weapons systems Hannah mentioned could have been designed, constructed, or operated without college-educated men proves that this is not just Fourth of July rhetoric. Hannah gives us an even better look at his idea of education in an article entitled, "The Schools' Responsibility in National Defense," where he comments: "I believe the primary and secondary schools can make education serve the individual and national interest by preparing youngsters for military service and life under conditions of stress as well as preparing them for college, or for a job or profession

11

. . . I would not even shrink from putting the word 'indoctrination' to the kind of education I have in mind. If we do not hesitate to indoctrinate our children with a love of truth, a love of home, and a love of God, then I see no justification for balking at teaching them love of country and love of what this country means."[13]

Hannah's comment about "life under conditions of stress" is related to a remark made by Eric A. Walker, president of Pennsylvania State University, a few years ago. There had been a series of student suicides and attempted suicides within a relatively short period of time. Many students and faculty members started grumbling about the newly instituted "term" system—a kind of "speed-up"—relating the stress and strain of the new system to the student suicides. Dr Walker's response to this unrest was to comment on how the increased pressure on the students was a good thing, since it enabled them to "have their nervous breakdowns early," before they graduated and had jobs and families when having a nervous breakdown would cause them more difficulties.

Despite the crass attitudes of so many of our educators, or the dehumanization of the form and content of our educational institutions, it would be a mistake to think the problems are only within the educational system. While it is true that education has been stripped of any meaning it once had, and Dr Conant is reduced to defining education as "what goes on in schools and colleges,"[14] our system of schools and colleges are far from a point of collapse. In fact, they are thriving. The "knowledge industry," as Kerr calls it, accounts for 30% of the Gross National Product; and, it is expanding at *twice* the rate of any sector of the economy. Schoolteachers make up the largest single occupational group of the labor force—some 3 million workers. Twenty-five years ago, the government and industry were hardly interested in education. But in 1960, the aggregate national outlay, public and private, amounted to 23.1 billions. As Kerr says, "the university has become a prime interest of national purpose. This is new. This is the essence of the transformation now engulfing our universities."[15] In short, our educational institutions are becoming appendages to, and transformed by, U.S. corporate capitalism.

Education is not being done away with in favor of something called training. Rather, education is being transformed from a quasi-aristocratic classicism and petit-bourgeois romanticism into something quite new. These changes are apparent in ways other than the quantitative statistics given above. For example, we can examine the social sciences and the humanities. The social and psychological "reality" that we are given to study is "objectified" to the point of sterility. The real world, we are to understand, is "value-free" and pragmatically bears little or no relation to the actual life-activity of men, classes, and nations. In one sense, we are being conditioned for life in a lifeless, stagnant, and sterile society.

For another example, there is more than a semantic connection between the academic division of labor and specialization we are all aware of and the corresponding division of labor that has gone on in large-scale industry. But it is important to understand what that connection is. It does *not* follow that because technology becomes diversified and specialized, then academic knowledge and skills must follow suit. Andre Gorz makes the relevant comment: "It is completely untrue that modern technology demands specialization: quite the reverse. It demands a basic 'polyvalent' education, comprising not a fragmentary, predigested and specialized knowledge, but an initiation—or, put more precisely, a faculty of self-initiation—into methods of scientifico-technological research and discovery."[16] If it is not the new technological production that deems necessary the kind of isolated specialization we know so well, then what is responsible? Gorz spells it out again: "Capitalism actually needs shattered and atomized men. . ."[17] in order to maintain its system of centralized, bureaucratized and militarized hierarchies, so as "to perpetuate its domination over men, not only as workers, but also as consumers and citizens."[18]

From this perspective, we can begin to understand that the educational malaise we as students and faculty have felt so personally and intensely is no aberration, but firmly rooted in the American political economy. In fact, the Organized System which Paul Goodman calls "compulsory mis-education" may mis-educate us, but it certainly serves the masters of that system, the U.S. ruling class, quite well. As Edgar Z. Friedenberg wrote: "Educational evils are attributed to *defective* schools. In fact, they are as likely to be the work of *effective* schools that are being directed toward evil ends by the society that supports and con-

13

trols them.''[19] Furthermore, he continues later in the same article, ''Schools are a definite indication that a society is divisible into a dominant and a subordinate group, and that the dominant group wants to teach the subordinate group something they could not be trusted to learn if left to themselves.''[20] Clark Kerr would accept this, both for the society in general, which he divides into ''managers'' and ''managed,'' and for the university. Kerr states: ''The intellectuals (including university students) are a particularly volatile element. . . They are by nature irresponsible. . . They are, as a result, never fully trusted by anybody, including themselves.''[21] But Kerr doesn't dismiss us. Even if we are by nature irresponsible (perhaps because we can perceive the contradictions?) he considers us essential: ''It is important who best attracts or captures the intellectuals and who uses them most effectively, for they may be a tool as well as a source of danger.''[22]

I think we can conclude that the American educational system is a coherent, well-organized, and—to the extent that the rulers are still ruling—effective mechanism. However, it has turned our humanitarian values into their opposites and at the same time, given us the potential to understand and critically evaluate both ourselves and the system itself. To that extent the system is fraught with internal contradictions. Furthermore, the events comprising the student revolt in the last few years demonstrate the likelihood that those contradictions will continue to manifest themselves in an open and protracted struggle. As Kerr predicted, we *are* a source of danger and incipient revolt. And the fact that Kerr was fired and the police used in the face of the revolt only goes to prove that those contradictions are irreconcilable within the structure of corporate capitalism. As Quinton Hoare remarked in *New Left Review* 32, ''a reform of the educational system involves a reform of the educators as well, and this is a political task, which immediately richochets back to the question of transforming consciousness and ideology throughout society.''[23] The central problem of radically transforming the educational system is that of the transformation of the teaching and learning body—the faculty and students. And this transformation, while it *begins* with the demands of the students' and teachers' work situation, cannot take place unless it occurs *within* and is organically connected *to* the practice of a mass radical *political* movement.

Part Two
THE POLITICAL ECONOMY OF THE MULTIVERSITY

The Knowledge Factory

What sense does it make to refer to the university as a factory? Is it just a good analogy? Or is there more to it than that? According to Kerr, "The university and segments of industry are becoming more and more alike."[24] He also informs us that, "The university is being called upon to . . . merge its activities with industry as never before. . . ."[25] Furthermore, in terms of control, the merger that Kerr speaks of seems to have been completed. According to a study by H.P. Beck, "Altogether the evidence of major university-business connections at high levels seems overwhelming. The numerous high positions of power in industry, commerce, and finance held by at least two-thirds of the governing boards of these 30 leading universities would appear to give a decisive majority more than ample grounds for identifying their personal interests with those of business."[26] Indeed, the boards of regents or trustees of almost every college and university in the country read off like corporation directories.

But it is not ample proof to call a university a factory merely because it is controlled by the same people who control industry. We must look deeper. Let us look at a relatively recent development within the U.S. political economy—the "innovation industry." This aspect of corporate capitalism, usually referred to as "R & D," Research and Development, has become a major industry. Since 1940 it has grown 27 times over; and, presently, accounts for approximately 5% of the overall federal budget.[27] What is important for us to see is that 20% of the work and production of the innovation industry is done *directly* within the university. In fact, it is this phenomenon that, since World War II, has been transforming the academic landscape into what we now call the "multiversity." Entirely new areas of work have been created—research assistants and technicians, industrial consultants, research promoters, contracting officers, and research project managers.

While research and development can be seen only as an adjunct to the real business of the university—teaching—the position it occupies is much more strategic. *"The men who teach in*

15

America's graduate schools determine for the rest of us not only what is true and what is false, but in a large measure what is 'done' and 'not done.' Since the graduate schools are usually a generation ahead of whatever segment of society they lead, their influence at any particular moment always looks modest. Over the years, however, they are perhaps the single most important source of innovation in society.'[28] And those innovations are important in more ways than we might think. According to Mills, ''Research for bureaucratic ends serves to make authority more effective and more efficient by providing information of use to authoritative planners.''[29] In the end the multiversity becomes the vanguard of the *status quo*, providing the know-how to gently usher in the New Order of 1984. The clearest manifestation of this trend can be seen in the sciences. Mills concludes: ''Science—historically started in the universities and connected rather informally with private industry—has now become officially established in, for, and by the military order.''[30]

As I remarked earlier, the services rendered by American education to corporate capitalism are evidenced by the academic division of labor. According to James Conant, over 1600 different academic degrees are possible within our diploma mills, most of which parallel the skill demands of the new technology. But it is important to note that not only is the division of labor increasing *within* the universities, but also is occurring *among* the universities. Just as different factories can produce different *kinds* of commodities, different universities produce different *kinds* of students. A type of educational ''pluralism'' has been developing over the last few decades. The traditional Ivy League schools shape the sons and daughters of the ruling class and the old middle class into the new ruling and managerial elites. The state colleges and universities develop the sons and daughters of the working class and the petit-bourgeoisie into the highly skilled sectors of the new working class, the middle sector white collar workers, and the traditional middle class professionals. Finally, the new community and junior colleges serve the increasing educational needs of, for the most part, the sons and daughters of the working class. This division of function both within and among our schools has a further strategic importance for radical organizing that I will comment on in Part Three of this paper.

So far, we have only seen the connection between the univer-

16

sities and the factories of industry in a secondary sense. It is true that there are parallels between the form and content of the educational system and large-scale industry. It is true that the same people determine the decision-making parameters of both systems. It is true that the non-teaching intellectual work—the innovation industry—produces a commodity directly consumed by industry. All of this is still not sufficient evidence to call our schools "factories," except in an analogous sense. Before we can draw that conclusion, we must look at the *primary* function of our educational system—the work of teaching and learning.

A factory is the locus of the machinery of production, social in character, where men work together to produce a commodity for consumption in the market place. At that point, the commodities are purchased either directly by the public or by other sectors of industry. Furthermore, if one is a radical, there are strategic criteria about factories to be considered as well. Is the work done in the factory *productive* work; *i.e.*, are the commodities produced both socially necessary and useful rather than inherently designed for waste, repression, and destruction? In other words, would work of the same nature, although transformed, be essential to a rational (*i.e.*, socialist) political economy? These are the sort of questions that must be dealt with before we can arrive at a radical understanding of both our educational system and the new characteristics of advanced industrial society.

Work and Alienation within the University

To begin, I will make a number of qualifications for the purpose of resolving disputes with other radicals before they happen. First of all, much of the work done in American education is irrational. Both the learning and teaching of many (but not all) of the manipulative techniques of bourgeois political economy that go on in our schools of business administration, education, and social science can in no sense be considered productive work. However, while this is true of the university in part, it does not follow that it is true of the university as an *objective whole*.

Second, I am not trying to say that students are workers in the strict sense. At best, so long as he, his family, or his friends are paying for his education, his learning activity results only in the

17

production of *use value*; *i.e.*, the potentially socially useful increase in the *future* productivity of his labor power. However, to the extent to which the student is *paid* by private or state institutions to engage in *specific* kinds of intellectual work, his activity *might in some cases* be seen as commodity production: *i.e.*, the development of the productivity of his labor power as an *actual exchange-value*, rather than as a potential use-value. This small number of students might be called workers. However, the position of most students is that of workers-to-be, *i.e.*, trainee or apprentice. But as a trainee, it is important that we recognize that many students share many of the social relations and conditions of production with many of the skilled workers of large-scale industry.

Finally, it is true that many faculty members are becoming more entrepreneurial and developing many interests that are objectively bound up with the ruling and sub-ruling classes. However, to say this is true of all faculty members fails to take into account a kind of class division that is occurring *within* the faculty in American universities. Clark Kerr distinguishes three functional types within the faculty of the multiversity.[31] The top level faculty—the heads of departments, intellectual administrators, research promoters, and paid consultants—should be seen as petty bourgeois and managerial sector constituents who have their interests tied up with the ruling and sub-ruling classes. The second group, the traditional academics, should be seen as middle-class professionals in the classic sense. However, the third and largest group, the lower-echelon faculty who are primarily engaged in teaching in the mass production line of large classes should be seen as members of the *new working class*. Their objective interests are with the students and the working class in general, despite the significant problem of false consciousness. This point is also of strategic and tactical importance and will be considered in Part Three.

So much for the qualifications. What is the nature of the teaching-learning activity within our educational institutions that might permit us to call them "knowledge factories" in other than an analogous sense? First of all, we need to take into account a few historical factors. The growth of the American political economy in the last thirty years has been facilitated in part by the development of a new technology. The development of the

18

new technology itself, the job displacements it created, and the increase in job skills required for its operation, created tremendous pressure on the state for the training of a highly skilled sector within the labor force. The working class, recognizing the need for the new skills, both for themselves and their children, also made demands of the government for both more and better education. Even at present, skill levels are rising at perhaps the highest rate in history. The government responded and is continuing to respond. According to Kerr, "Higher education in 1960 received about 1.5 billion from the federal government—a *hundredfold* increase in twenty years."[32] However, while the demand for expanding education comes from both the needs of a developing technology and from the demands of working class parents, it is the needs of the industrialists that *structure* the form and content of the educational expansion. According to Gorz, the state responds to capital rather than people, "since the development of education falls under the general head of growing *collective* needs produced by monopolistic expansion. . . ."[33] In the last few decades, the expanding reproduction and accumulation of a continuing increase in the *productivity of labor power* is an *objective necessity* of contemporary corporate capitalism. Kerr remarks: "Instead of waiting outside the gates, agents [of the industrialists] are working the corridors. They also work the placement offices."[34]

The colleges and universities have gone beyond their traditional task of socialization and acculturation. They are deeply involved in the production of a crucial and marketable commodity—labor power. Again Gorz comments: "the work of learning (and teaching) of extending and transforming professional skills is implicitly recognized as socially necessary and productive work, through which the individual transforms *himself* according to the needs of society (and industry). . . ."[35] It is *this* aspect of the university that is the most crucial for the political economy. The production of an increase in socially useful and necessary labor power is the new historic function of our educational institutions that enables us to name them, quite accurately, *knowledge factories*. In this process of historical change, liberal education has been transformed into its opposite, and what we are witnessing is the advent of training and indoctrination. The core of the university, with its frills removed, has become the crucible for the pro-

19

duction, formation, and socialization of the new working class.

What does the interior of the new knowledge factory look like? Where are the workshops? Specifically, these are to be found in the classrooms, the faculty offices, the study rooms in the libraries and homes, the psychological counseling offices and clinics, the conference rooms, the research laboratories, and the administrative staff offices. What kind of machinery can we find in these mental sweatshops? What kind of apparatus have our rulers constructed in the name of our enlightenment? The machinery of knowledge-production pervades the university. And, despite its apparent invisibility, it is no less real or tangible. The productive apparatus consists of grades, exams, assigned books, papers, and reports, all the curriculum and scheduling requirements, non-academic *in loco parentis* regulations, scientific equipment and resources, the mechanics of grants and endowments, disciplinary procedures, campus and civil police, and all the repressive and sublimative psychological techniques of fear and punishment. Most, if not all, of this machinery and the purpose it is used for are beyond the control of the students and the faculty who work with it. All government, all control, all the parameters of decision-making have fallen into the hands of the adminstrative representatives of the ruling class. At best, hand-picked ''representatives'' of student and faculty ''opinion'' are pre-arranged. For example, female students are permitted to determine how strict or ''liberal'' their dorm hours might be; but the underlying assumption of whether they should have curfews at all is beyond question. Or, while some (but not all) college professors are free to teach *what* they please, they are not ''free to decide *how* to teach—whether in large numbers or small, in departmentalized courses or others, one day a week or five.''[36]

In the past the work of teaching and learning was a two-way process with the Socratic dialectic as its purest form. However, with the advent of the corporate state and its corresponding appropriation of the cultural apparatus, education has become increasingly one-dimensional. Teaching is reduced to an uncritical *distribution* of pre-established skills, techniques and ''data,'' while learning is transformed into the passive *consumption* of the same. In its broadest sense, culture—that which is man-made—is turned into its opposite—anti-culture—the creature of expanding production. Education, meaning ''to educe,'' to draw out from, has

20

become something that the state *gives* to people. Finally, teacher and students, both dehumanized distributors and consumers of the knowledge commodity, become commodities themselves—something to be bought and sold in the university placement office.

But it is not enough for the knowledge factory to produce skilled labor power in the form of a *raw material*. The commodity must be socially useful as well. When describing the multiversity's machinery Clark Kerr tells us that academic processes and requirements are "part of the process of freezing the structure of the occupational pyramid and assuring that *the well-behaved do advance even if the geniuses do not* (emphasis mine)."[37] Our rough edges must be worn off, our spirit broken, our hopes mundane, and our manners subservient and docile. And if we won't pacify and repress ourselves with all the mechanisms *they* have constructed for our self-flagellation, the police will be called.

Like any good training program, the knowledge factory accurately reproduces all the conditions and relations of production in the factories of advanced corporate capitalism—isolation, manipulation, and alienation. First, the teaching and learning workers of the knowledge factory are alienated from each other, isolated and divided among themselves by grades, class ranks, and the status levels of the bureaucratic hierarchy. Secondly, they are alienated from the product of their work, the content and purpose of which have been determined and used by someone other than themselves. Finally, they are alienated in the activity of education itself. What should be the active creation and re-creation of culture is nothing more than forced and coercive consumption and distribution of data and technique. Throughout the educational apparatus, the bureaucratic mentality prevails. History and ideology have come to an end. Science, the humanities, even philosophy have become value-free. Politics are reduced to advertising and sales campaigns. Finally, government and self-determination become matters of administration and domination.

The Meaning of the Student Revolt

Our manipulators have overlooked one fundamental factor; there is one facet of human history to which the bureaucratic *Weltanschauung* is blind. *Men are not made of clay.* Despite all the official pronouncements asserting the end of this or that, the well-

21

springs of human freedom still run deep. All the attempts to teach ignorance in the place of knowledge have come to naught. The student revolt is an historic event. Someone (the Berkeley students?) let the cat out of the bag. The emperor has no clothes.

Our rulers are aware of this. The bureaucrats of corporate capitalism must cut back and control the quality and content of "liberal" education. They know only too well that a widespread culture rising out of critical thought might challenge, during a crisis, the existing relations of production and domination. The CIA control of the NSA [National Student Association] and other "cultural" organizations proves this only too well.

But the corporate ruling class is not primarily interested in containing and pacifying us *as intellectuals*. Their real concern with us lies in our role as the highly skilled members of the new working class. As Gorz points out, "skilled workers. . . possess *in their own right. . .* the labor power they lend."[38] Their skills are an attribute of *themselves* and not just the material means of production. Gorz continues: "the problem of big management is to harmonize two contradictory necessities: the necessity of developing human capabilities, imposed by modern processes of production and the political necessity of insuring that this kind of development does not bring in its wake any augmentation of the independence of the individual, provoking him to challenge the present division of social labor and distribution of power."[39]

From this analysis, we can understand the student revolt in its most strategic and crucial sense. What we are witnessing and participating in is an important historical phenomenon: the revolt of the trainees of the new working class against the alienated and oppressive conditions of production and consumption within corporate capitalism. These are the conditions of life and activity that lie beneath the apathy, frustration, and rebellion on America's campuses. Andre Gorz predicted a few years back: "It is in education that industrial capitalism will provoke revolts which it attempts to avoid in its factories."[40]

Nevertheless, the "student power" movement is still vague and undefined. Its possibilities are hopeful as well as dangerous. On the one hand, student power can develop into an elitist corporate monster, mainly concerned with developing better techniques of "co-managing" the bureaucratic apparatus of advanced industrial society. On the other hand, a student power movement might successfully develop a revolutionary class consciousness among the future new working class, who would organize on their jobs and among the traditional working class around the issues of participatory democracy and worker control. The character of the future movement will depend a great extent on the kind of strategy and tactics we use in the present. The struggle will be protracted, that is certain. There is no certain or pre-determined victory. We should not forget that *1984* is possible. And not many years away. But we have several years of experience behind us from which we can learn a great deal.

Part Three
THE PRAXIS OF STUDENT POWER
STRATEGY AND TACTICS

Socialism on One Campus: An Infantile Disorder

Perhaps the single most important factor for the student power movement to keep in mind is the fact that the university is intimately bound up with the society in general. Because of this, we should always remember that we cannot liberate the university without radically changing the rest of society. The lesson to be drawn is that any attempt to build a student movement based on "on-campus" issues only is inherently conservative and ultimately reactionary. Every attempt should be made to connect campus issues with off-campus questions. For example, the question of ranking and university complicity with the Selective Service System needs to be tied to a general anti-draft and "No Draft for Vietnam" movement. The question of the presence of the military on the campus in all its forms needs to be tied to the question of what the military is used for—fighting aggressive wars of oppression abroad—and not just to the question of secret research being poor academic policy. Furthermore, the student movement must actively seek to join off-campus struggles in the surrounding community. For example, strikes by local unions should be supported if possible. This kind of communication and understanding with the local working class is essential if we are ever going to have community support for student strikes.

23

Radicalizing the New Working Class

If there is a single over-all purpose for the student power movement, it would be the development of a radical political consciousness among those students who will later hold jobs in strategic sectors of the political economy. This means that we should reach out to engineers and technical students rather than to business administration majors, education majors rather than to art students. From a national perspective, this strategy would also suggest that we should place priorities on organizing in certain *kinds* of universities—the community colleges, junior colleges, state universities, and technical schools, rather than religious colleges or the Ivy League.

One way to mount political action around this notion is to focus on the placement offices—the nexus between the university and industry. For example, when Dow Chemical comes to recruit, our main approach to junior and senior chemical engineering students who are being interviewed should not only be around the issue of the immorality of napalm. Rather, our leaflets should say that one of the main faults of Dow and all other industries as well, is that their workers *have no control* over content or purposes of their work. In other words, Dow Chemical is bad, not only because of napalm, but mainly because it renders its workers *powerless*, makes them *unfree*. In short, Dow and all American industry oppresses *its own workers* as well as the people of the Third World. Dow in particular should be run off the campus and students urged not to work for them because of their complicity in war crimes. But when other industries are recruiting, our leaflets should address themselves to the interviewees' instincts of workmanship, his desire to be free and creative, to do humane work, rather than work for profit. We should encourage him, if he takes the job, to see himself in this light—as a skilled worker—and to see his self-interest in organizing on his future job with his fellow workers, skilled and unskilled, for control of production and the end to which his work is directed. The need for control, for the power, on and off the job, to affect the decisions shaping one's life in all arenas; developing this kind of consciousness, on and off the campus, is what we should be fundamentally about.

Practical, Critical Activity: Notes on Organizing

There are three virtues necessary for successful radical organizing: honesty, patience, and a sense of humor. First of all, if the students we are trying to reach can't trust us, who can they trust? Secondly, it takes time to build a movement. Sometimes several years of groundwork must be laid before a student power movement has a constituency. It took most of us several years before we had developed a radical perspective. Why should it be any different for the people we are trying to reach? This is not to say that everyone must repeat all the mistakes we have gone through, but there are certain *forms* of involvement and action that many students will have to repeat. Finally, by a sense of humor, I mean we must be life-affirming. Lusty passionate people are the only kind of men who have the enduring strength to motivate enough people to radically transform a life-negating system.

Che Guevara remarked in *Guerrilla Warfare* that as long as people had faith in certain institutions and forms of political activity, then the organizer must work *with* the people *through* those institutions, even though we might think those forms of action are dead ends.[41] The point of Che's remark is that people must learn that those forms are stacked against them through their *own experience* in attempting change. The role of the organizer at this point is crucial. He or she should neither passively go along with the student government "reformer" types nor stand apart from the action denouncing it as "sell-out." Rather, his task is that of *constant criticism* from within the action. When the reformers fail, become bogged down, or are banging their heads against the wall, the organizer should be there as *one who has been with them throughout their struggle* to offer the relevant analysis of *why* their approach has failed and to indicate future strategies and tactics.

However, we also need to be discriminating. There are certain forms of political action, like working with the Democratic Party, that are so obviously bankrupt, that we need not waste our time. In order to discern these limits, an organizer has to develop a sensitivity to understand where people are. Many radical actions have failed on campuses because the activists have failed in laying a base for a particular action. It does no good to sit in against the CIA if a broad educational campaign, petitions, and rallies on the nature of the CIA have not been done for several days before the sit-in. It is not enough that we have a clear understanding of the oppressiveness of institutions like the CIA and HUAC* before we act in a radical fashion. We must make our position clear to the students, faculty, and the surrounding community.

The Cultural Apparatus and the Problem of False Consciousness

In addition to its role in the political economy, it is important to deal with the university as the backbone of what Mills called "the cultural apparatus."[42] He defined this as all those organizations and *milieux* in which artistic, scientific and intellectual work goes on, as well as the means by which that work is made available to others. Within this apparatus, the various vehicles of communication—language, the mass arts, public arts, and design arts—stand between a man's consciousness and his material existence. At present, the bulk of the apparatus is centralized and controlled by the corporate rulers of America. As a result, their use of the official communications has the effect of limiting our experience and, furthermore, expropriates much of that potential experience that we might have called our own. What we need to understand is that the cultural apparatus, properly used, has the ability both to transform power into authority and transform authority into mere overt coercion.

At present, the university's role in acculturation and socialization is the promulgation of the utter mystification of "corporate consciousness." Society is presented to us as a kind of caste system in which we are to see ourselves as a "privileged elite"—a bureaucratic man channeled into the proper bureaucratic niche. In addition to strengthening the forms of social control off the campus, the administration uses the apparatus to legitimize its own power over us.

On the campus, the student press, underground newspapers, campus radio and television, literature tables, posters and leaflets, artist and lecture series, theaters, films, and the local press make up a good part of the non-academic cultural media. Most of it is both actively and passively being used against us. Any student power movement should 1) try to gain control of as much of the *established* campus cultural apparatus as possible; 2) if control

* HUAC, the House Un-American Activities Committee (now defunct), was a government witch-hunting body that specialized in investigation and harassment of labor activists and other leftists (Publisher's Note).

26

is not possible, we should try to influence and/or resist it when necessary; and 3) organize and develop a new counter-apparatus of our own. In short, we need our people on the staff of the school newspapers and radio stations. We need our own local magazines. We need sympathetic contacts on local off-campus news media. Finally, we all could use some training in graphic and communicative arts.

What this all adds up to is strengthening our ability to wage an effective "de-sanctification" program against the authoritarian institutions controlling us. The purpose of de-sanctification is to strip institutions of their legitimizing authority, to have them reveal themselves to the people under them for what they are—raw coercive power. This is the purpose of singing the Mickey Mouse Club jingle at student government meetings, of ridiculing and harrassing student disciplinary hearings and tribunals, of burning the Dean of Men and/or Women in effigy. People will not move *against* institutions of power until the legitimizing authority has been stripped away. On many campuses this has already happened; but for those remaining, the task remains. And we should be forewarned: it is a tricky job and often can backfire, delegitimizing us.

The Correct Handling of Student Governments

While student governments vary in form in the United States, the objective reasons for their existence are the containment, or pacification and manipulation of the student body. Very few of our student governments are autonomously incorporated or have any powers or rights apart from those sanctioned by the regents or trustees of the university. Furthermore, most administrations hold a veto power over anything done by the student governments. Perhaps the worst aspect of this kind of manipulation and repression is that the administration uses students to control other students. Most student government politicos are lackeys of the worst sort. That is, they have internalized and embraced all the repressive mechanisms the administration has designed for use *against* them and their fellow students.

With this in mind, it would seem that we should ignore student governments and/or abolish them. While this is certainly true in the final analysis, it is important to relate to student governments differently during the earlier stages of on-campus political struggles. The question we are left with is how do we render student governments ineffective in terms of what they are designed to do, while at the same time, using them effectively in building the movement?

Do we work inside the system? Of course we do. The question is not one of working "inside" or "outside" the system. Rather, the question is: Do we play by the established rules? Here, the answer is an emphatic no. The established habits of student politics—popularity contest elections, disguising oneself as a moderate, working for "better communications and dialogue" with administrators, watering down demands before they are made, going through channels—all of these gambits are stacked against us. If liberal and moderate student politicians really believe in them, then we should tell *them* to try it with all they have. But if they continue to make this ploy after they have learned from their own experience that these methods are dead-ends, then they should be soundly denounced as opportunists or gutless administration puppets.

We should face the fact that student governments are *powerless* and designed to stay that way. From this perspective, all talk about "getting into power" is so much nonsense. The only thing that student governments are useful for is their ability to be a *temporary vehicle* in building a grass-roots student power movement. This means that student elections are useful as an arena for raising real issues, combatting and exposing administration apologists, and involving new people, rather than getting elected. If our people do happen to get elected *as radicals* (this is becoming increasingly possible) then the seats won should be used as a focal point and sounding board for demonstrating the impotence of student government *from within*. A seat should be seen as a soap-box, where our representatives can stand, gaining a kind of visibility and speaking to the student body as a whole, over the heads of the other student politicians.

Can anything positive be gained through student government? Apart from publicity, one thing it can be used for is money. Many student-activities funds are open for the kinds of things we would like to see on campus: certain speakers, films, sponsoring conferences. Money, without strings, is always a help. Also, non-political services such as non-profit used-book exchanges, are helpful to many students. But in terms of radical changes, student government can do nothing apart from a mass, radical student power movement. Even then, student government tends to be a conservative force within those struggles. In the end, meaningful changes can only come through a radical transformation of both the consciousness of large numbers of students and the forms of student self-government.

Reform or Revolution:
What Kinds of Demands?

Fighting for reforms and making a revolution should not be seen as mutually exclusive positions. The question should be: What kind of reforms move us toward a radical transformation of both the university and the society in general? First of all, we should avoid the kinds of reforms which leave the basic *rationale* of the system unchallenged. For instance, a bad reform to work for would be getting a better grading system, because the underlying rationale—the need for grades at all—remains unchallenged.

Secondly, we should avoid certain kinds of reform that divide students from each other. For instance, trying to win certain privileges for upper classmen but not for freshmen or sophomores. Or trying to establish non-graded courses for students above a certain grade-point average. In the course of campus political activity, the administration will try a whole range of "divide and rule" tactics such as fostering the "Greek-Independent Split," sexual double standards, intellectual vs. "jocks," responsible vs. irresponsible leaders, redbaiting and "non-student" vs. students. We need to avoid falling into these traps ahead of time, as well as fighting them when used against us.

Finally, we should avoid all of the "co-management" kinds of reforms. These usually come in the form of giving certain "responsible" student leaders a voice or influence in certain decision-making processes, rather than abolishing or winning effective control over those parts of the governing apparatus. One way to counter administration suggestions for setting up "tripartite" committees (1/3 student, 1/3 faculty, 1/3 administration, each with an equal number of votes) is to say, "OK, but once a month the committee must hold an all-university plenary session—one man, one vote." The thought of being outvoted 1000 to 1 will cause administrators to scrap that co-optive measure in a hurry.

29

We have learned the hard way that the reformist path is full of pitfalls. What, then, are the kinds of reformist measures that do make sense? First of all, there are the civil libertarian issues. We must always fight, dramatically and quickly, for free speech and the right to organize, advocate, and mount political action—of all sorts. However, even here, we should avoid getting bogged down in "legalitarianism." We cannot count on this society's legal apparatus to guarantee our civil liberties: and, we should not organize around civil libertarian issues *as if it could*. Rather, when our legal rights are violated, we should move as quickly as possible, without losing our base, to expand the campus libertarian moral indignation into a multi-issues *political* insurgency, exposing the repressive character of the administration and the corporate state in general.

The second kind of partial reform worth fighting for and possibly winning is the abolition of on-campus repressive mechanisms, *i.e.*, student courts, disciplinary tribunals, deans of men and women, campus police, and the use of civil police on campus. While it is true that "abolition" is a negative reform, and while we will be criticized for not offering "constructive" criticisms, we should reply that the only constructive way to deal with an inherently destructive apparatus is to destroy it. We must curtail the ability of administrators to repress our *need to refuse* their way of life—the regimentation and bureaucratization of existence.

When our universities are already major agencies for social change in the direction of *1984*, our initial demands must, almost of necessity, be negative demands. In this sense, the first task of student power movement will be the organization of a holding action—a resistance. Along these lines, one potentially effective tactic for resisting the university's disciplinary apparatus would be the formation of a Student Defense League. The purpose of the group would be to make its services available to any student who must appear before campus authorities for infractions of repressive (or just plain stupid) rules and regulations. The defense group would then attend the student's hearings *en masse*. However, for some cases, it might be wise to include law students or local radical lawyers in the group for the purpose of making legal counter-attacks. A student defense group would have three major goals: 1) saving as many students as possible from punishment, 2) de-sanctifying and rendering dis-functional the administration's repressive apparatus, and 3) using 1) and 2) as tactics in reaching other students for building a movement to abolish the apparatus as a whole.

When engaging in this kind of activity, it is important to be clear in our rhetoric as to what we are about. We are not trying to *liberalize* the existing order, but trying to win our *liberation* from it. We must refuse the administrations' rhetoric of "responsibility." To their one-dimensional way of thinking, the concept of responsibility has been reduced to its opposite, namely, be nice, don't rock the boat, do things according to *our* criteria of what is permissible. In actuality their whole system is geared toward the inculcation of the values of a planned irresponsibility. We should refuse *their* definitions, *their* terms, and even refuse to engage in *their* semantic hassles. We only need to define for *ourselves and other students* our notions of what it means to be free, constructive, and responsible. Too many campus movements have been co-opted for weeks or even permanently by falling into the administrations' rhetorical bags.

Besides the abolition of repressive disciplinary mechanisms within the university, there are other negative reforms that radicals should work for. Getting the military off the campus, abolishing the grade system, and abolishing universal compulsory courses (*i.e.*, physical education) would fit into this category. However, an important question for the student movement is whether or not *positive* radical reforms can be won within the university short of making a revolution in the society as a whole. Furthermore, would the achievement of these kinds of partial reforms have the cumulative effect of weakening certain aspects of corporate capitalism, and, in their small way, make that broader revolution more likely?

At present, my feeling is that these kinds of anti-capitalist positive reforms are almost as hard to conceive intellectually as they are to win. To be sure, there has been a wealth of positive educational reforms suggested by people like Paul Goodman. But are they anti-capitalist as well? For example, we have been able to organize several good free universities. Many of the brightest and most sensitive students on American campuses, disgusted with the present state of education, left the campus and organized these counter-institutions. Some of their experiments were successful in an immediate internal sense. A few of these organizers were initially convinced that the sheer moral force of their work in these free institutions would cause the existing educational structure to tremble and finally collapse like a house of IBM cards. But what happened? What effect did the free universities have on the established educational order? At best, they had no effect. But it is more likely that they had the effect of strengthening the existing system. How? First of all, the best of our people left the campus, enabling the existing university to function more smoothly, since the "troublemakers" were gone. Secondly, they gave liberal administrators the rhetoric, the analysis, and sometimes the man-power to co-opt their programs and establish elitist forms of "experimental" colleges inside of, although quarantined from, the existing educational system. This is not to say that free universities should not be organized, both on and off the campus. They can be valuable and useful. But they should not be seen as a primary aspect of a strategy for change.

What then is open to us in the area of positive anti-capitalist reforms? For the most part, it will be difficult to determine whether or not a reform has the effect of being anti-capitalist until it has been achieved. Since it is both difficult and undesirable to attempt to predict the future, questions of this sort are often best answered in practice. Nevertheless, it would seem that the kind of reforms we are looking for are most likely to be found within a strategy of what I would call "encroaching control." There are aspects of the university's administrative, academic, financial, physical, and social apparatus that are potentially, if not actually, useful and productive. While we should try to abolish the repressive mehanisms of the university, our strategy should be to gain *control*, piece by piece, of its positive aspects.

What would that control look like? To begin, all aspects of the non-academic life of the campus should either be completely under the control of the students as individuals or embodied in the institutional forms *they* establish for their collective government. For example, an independent union of students should have the final say on the form and content of *all-university* political, social, and cultural events. Naturally, individual students and student organizations would be completely free in organizing events of their own.

Second, only the students and the teaching faculty, individually and through their organizations, should control the academic affairs of the university. One example of a worthwhile reform in this area would be enabling all history majors and history professors to meet jointly at the beginning of each semester and shape the form, content, and direction of their departmental curriculum. Another partial reform in this area would be enabling an independent union of students to hire additional professors of their choice and establish additional accredited courses of their choice independently of the faculty or administration.

Finally, we should remember that control should be sought *for some specific purpose*. One reason we want this kind of power is to enable us to meet the *self-determined* needs of students and teachers. But another objective that we should see as radicals is to put as much of the university's resources as possible into the hands of the underclass and the working class. We should use the student press to publicize and support local strikes. We should use campus facilities for meeting the educational needs of insurgent organizations of the poor, and of the rank and file workers. Or we could mobilize the universities' research facilities for serving projects established and controlled by the poor and workers, rather than projects established and controlled by the government, management, and labor bureaucrats. The conservative nature of American trade unions makes activity of this sort very difficult, although not impossible. But we should always be careful to make a distinction between the American working class and the labor bureaucrats.

The Faculty Question: Allies or Finks?

One question almost always confronts the student movement on the campus. Do we try to win faculty support before we go into action? Or do we lump them together with the administration? What we have learned in the past seems to indicate that both of these responses are wrong. Earlier in this paper, I remarked on the kinds of divisions that exist among the faculty. What is important to see is that this division is not just between good and bad guys. Rather, the faculty is becoming more and more divided in terms of the objective functions of their jobs. To make the hard case on the one hand, the function of the lower level of the faculty is to teach—a potentially creative and useful activity; on

33

the other hand, the function of most administrative and research faculty is manipulation, repression, and—for the defense department hirelings—destruction. In general, we should develop our strategies so that our lot falls with the teaching faculty and theirs with ours. As for the research and administrative faculty, we should set both ourselves and the teaching faculty against them. Also, during any student confrontation with the administration, the faculty can do one of four things *as a group*. They can 1) support the administration, 2) remain neutral, 3) split among themselves, or 4) support us. In any situation, we should favor the development of one of the last three alternatives rather than the first. Furthermore, if it seems likely that the faculty will split on an issue, we should try to encourage the division indicated above. While it is important to remain open to the faculty, we should not let their support or non-support become an issue in determining whether or not we begin to mount political action. Finally, we should encourage the potentially radical sectors of the faculty to organize among themselves around their own grievances, hopefully being able to *eventually* form a radical alliance with us.

The Vital Issue of Teaching Assistants' Unions

Probably the most exploited and alienated group of people on any campus *are* the graduate student teaching assistants. The forces of the multiversity hit them from two directions—both as students and as teachers. As students, they have been around long enough to have lost their awe of academia. As faculty, they are given the worst jobs for the lowest pay. For the most part, they have no illusions about their work. Their working conditions, low pay, and the fact that their futures are subject to the whimsical machinations of their department chairmen, make them a group ripe for radical organization. Furthermore, their strategic position within the university structure makes them potentially powerful as a group if they should decide to organize and strike. If they go out, a large part of the multiversity comes grinding to a halt. The kinds of demands they are most likely to be organized around naturally connect them with a radical student power movement and with the potentially radical sector of the faculty. Furthermore, these considerations make the organization of a radical trade union

34

of TAs a crucial part of any strategy for change. We should see this kind of labor organizing as one of our first priorities in building the campus movement.

Non-academic Employees:
On-campus Labor Organizing

Almost all colleges and especially the multiversities have a large number of blue-collar maintenance workers on campus. Within the state-supported institutions in particular, these people are often forbidden to organize unions, have terrible working conditions, and are paid very low wages. Their presence on the campus offers a unique opportunity for many students to become involved in blue-collar labor organizing at the same time that they are in school. Secondly, since these workers usually live in the surrounding community, their friends and relatives will come from other sectors of the local working class. Quite naturally, they will carry their ideas, opinions, and feelings toward the radical student movement home with them. In this sense, they can be an important link connecting us with other workers, and our help in enabling them to organize a local independent and radical trade union would help tremendously. Finally, if we should ever strike as students, they could be an important ally. For instance, after SDS at the University of Missouri played a major role in organizing a militant local of non-academic employees, they learned that, were the union to strike for its own demands in sympathy with student demands, the university as a physical plant would cease to function after four days. It is obviously important to have that kind of power.

The Knowledge Machinery and Sabotage:
Striking on the Job

One mistake radical students have been making in relating to the worst aspects of the multiversity's academic apparatus has been their avoidance of it. We tend to avoid large classes, lousy courses, and reactionary professors like the plague. At best, we have organized counter-courses outside the classroom and off the campus. My suggestion is that we should do the opposite. Our brightest people should sign up for the large freshman and sophomore sections with the worst profs in *strategic* courses in history, political science, education, and even the ROTC counter-insurgency lectures. From this position, they should then begin to take out their frustration with the work of the course while they are on the job, *i.e.*, inside the classroom. Specifically, they should be constant vocal critics of the form and content of the course, the prof, class size, the educational system, and corporate capitalism in general. Their primary strategy, rather than winning debating points against the prof, should be to reach other students in the class. Hopefully, our on-the-job organizer will begin to develop a radical caucus in the class. This group could then meet outside of the class, continue to collectively develop a further radical critique of the future classwork, to be presented at the succeeding sessions. If all goes well with the prof, and perhaps his department as well, they will have a full-scale academic revolt on their hands by the end of the semester. Finally, if this sort of work were being done in a variety of courses at once, the local radical student movement would have the makings of an underground educational movement that was actively engaged in mounting an effective resistance to the educational *status quo*.

Provo Tactics: Radicalization or Sublimation?

There is little doubt that the hippie movement has made its impact on most American campuses. It is also becoming more clear that the culture of advanced capitalist society is becoming more sterile, dehumanized and one-dimensional. It is directed toward a passive mass, rather than an active public. Its root value is consumption. We obviously need a cultural revolution, along with a revolution in the political economy. But the question remains: where do the hippies fit in? At the present time, their role seems ambivalent.

On the one hand, they thoroughly reject the dominant culture and seem to be life-affirming. On the other hand, they seem to be for the most part passive consumers of culture, rather than active creators of culture. For all their talk of community, the nexus of their relations with each other seems to consist only of drugs and a common jargon. With all their talk of love, one finds little deep-rooted passion. Yet, they are there; and they are a major phenomenon. Their relevance to the campus scene is evidenced by the success of the wave of "Gentle Thursdays" that swept the

36

country. Through this approach, we have been able to reach and break loose a good number of people. Often, during the frivolity of Gentle Thursday, the life-denying aspects of corporate capitalism are brought home to many people with an impact that could never be obtained by the best of all of our anti-war demonstrations.

However, the hippie movement has served to make many of our people withdraw into a personalistic, passive cult of consumption. These aspects need to be criticized and curtailed. We should be clear about one thing: the *individual* liberation of man, the most social of animals, is a dead-end—an impossibility. And even if individual liberation were possible, would it be desirable? The sublimation of reality within the individual consciousness neither destroys nor transforms the objective reality of other men.

Nevertheless, the excitement and imagination of some aspects of hippiedom can be useful in building critiques of the existing culture. Here, I am referring to the provos and the diggers. Gentle Thursdays, when used as a provo (provocative) tactic on campus, can cause the administration to display some of its most repressive characteristics. Even something as blunt as burning a television set in the middle of campus can make a profound statement about the life-styles of many people. However, people engaging in these kind of tactics should 1) not see the action as a substitute for serious revolutionary activity and 2) read up on the Provos and the Situationists rather than the Haight-Ashbury scene.

From Soap-box to Student Strikes: The Forms of Protest

During the development of radical politics on the campus, the student movement will pass through a multitude of organizational forms. I have already mentioned several: Student Defense League, Teaching Assistants' Unions, Non-academic Employees' Unions, and of course, SDS chapters. Another important development on many campuses has been the formation of Black Student Unions, or Afro-American cultural groups. All of these groups are vital, although some are more important than others at different stages of the struggle. However, for the purpose of keeping a radical and multi-issue focus throughout the growth of the movement, it is important to begin work on a campus by organizing an SDS chapter.

37

From this starting point, how does SDS see its relation to the rest of the campus? I think we have learned that we should not look upon ourselves as an intellectual and political oasis, hugging each other in a wasteland. Rather, our chapters should see themselves as *organizing committees* for reaching out to the majority of the student population. Furthermore, we are organizing for something—the power to effect change. With this in mind, we should be well aware of the fact that the kind of power and changes we would like to have and achieve are not going to be given to us gracefully. Ultimately, we have access to only one source of power within the knowledge factory. And that power lies in our potential ability to stop the university from functioning, to render the system dysfunctional for limited periods of time. Throughout all our on-campus organizing efforts we should keep this one point in mind: that sooner or later we are going to have to strike—or at least successfully threaten to strike. Because of this, our constant strategy should be the preparation of a mass base for supporting and participating in this kind of action.

What are the organizational forms, other than those mentioned above, that are necessary for the development of this kind of radical constituency? The first kind of extra-SDS organization needed is a Hyde Park or Free Speech Forum. An area of the campus, centrally located and heavily traveled, should be selected and equipped with a P.A. system. Then, on a certain afternoon one day a week, the platform would be open to anyone to give speeches on anything they choose. SDS people should attend regularly and speak regularly, although they should encourage variety and debate, and not monopolize the platform. To begin, the forum should be weekly, so that students don't become bored with it. Rather, we should try to give it the aura of a special event. Later on, when political activity intensifies, the forum could be held every day. In the early stages, publicity, the establishment of a mood and climate for radical politics, is of utmost importance. We should make our presence felt everywhere—in the campus news media, leafleting and poster displays, and regular attendance at the meetings of all student political, social, and religious organizations. We should make all aspects of our politics as visible and open as possible.

Once our presence has become known, we can begin to organize on a variety of issues. One arena that it will be important to relate to at this stage will be student government elections. The best organizational form for this activity would be the formation of a Campus Freedom Party for running radical candidates. It is important that the party be clear and open as to its radical consciousness, keeping in mind that our first task is that of building radical consciousness, rather than winning seats. It is also important that the party take positions on off-campus questions as well, such as the war in Vietnam. Otherwise, if we only relate to on-campus issues, we run the risk of laying the counter-revolutionary groundwork for an elitist, conservative and corporatist student movement. As many people as possible should be involved in the function of the party, with SDS people having the function of keeping it militant and radical in a non-manipulative and honest fashion. The party should permeate the campus with speeches, films, and leaflets, as well as a series of solidly intellectual and radical position papers on a variety of issues. Furthermore, we should remember that an election campaign should be fun. Campus Freedom Parties should organize Gentle Thursdays, jug bands, rock groups, theater groups for political skits, and homemade 8mm. campaign films. Finally, during non-election periods, the Campus Freedom Party should form a variety of CFP *ad hoc* committees for relating to student government on various issues throughout the year.

The next stage of the movement is the most crucial and delicate: the formation of a Student Strike Coordinating Committee. There are two pre-conditions necessary for its existence. First, there must be a quasi-radical base of some size that has been developed from past activity. Secondly, either a crisis situation provoked by the administration or a climate of active frustration with the administration and/or the ruling class it represents must exist. The frustration should be centered around a set of specific demands that have been unresolved through the established channels of liberal action. If this kind of situation exists, then a strike is both possible and desirable. A temporary steering committee should be set up, consisting of representatives of radical groups (SDS, Black Student Union, TA's Union). This group would set the initial demands and put out the call for a strike within a few weeks' time. Within that time, they would try to bring in as many other groups and individuals as possible without seriously watering down the demands. This new coalition would then constitute itself

39

as the Student Strike Coordinating Committee, with the new groups adding members to the original temporary steering committee. Also, a series of working committees and a negotiating committee should be established. Finally, the strike committee should attempt to have as many open mass plenary sessions as possible.

What should come out of a student strike? First, the development of a radical consciousness among large numbers of students. Secondly, we should try to include within our demands some issues on which we can win partial victories. Finally, the organizational form that should grow out of a strike or a series of strikes is an independent, radical, and political Free Student Union that would replace the existing student government.

I have already dealt with the general political life of radical movements. But some points need to be repeated. First of all, a radical student union *must* be in alliance with the radical sectors of the underclass and working class. Secondly, the student movement has the additional task of radicalizing the sub-sector of the labor force that some of us in SDS have come to call the new working class. Thirdly, a radical union of students should have an anti-imperialist critique of U.S. foreign policy. Finally, local student unions, if they are to grow and thrive, must become federated on regional, national, and international levels.

However, we should be careful not to form a national union of students lacking in a grassroots constituency that actively and democratically participates in all aspects of the organization's life. One NSA is enough. On the international level, we should avoid both the CIA and Soviet-Union-sponsored International Unions. We would be better off to establish informal relations with groups like the Zengakuren in Japan, the German SDS, the French Situationists, the Spanish Democratic Student Syndicate, and the third world revolutionary student organizations. Hopefully, in the not too distant future, we may be instrumental in forming a new International Union of Revolutionary Youth. But there is much work to be done between now and then. And even greater tasks remain to be done before we can begin to build the conditions for human liberation.

NOTES

1) Marx: *Theses on Feuerbach*   2) *New York Times*, November 29, 1964
3) Kerr, Clark: *Uses of the University*, p. 103   4) Ibid., p. 101
5) Baran and Sweezy: *Monopoly Capital*
6) Golin, Steve: *New Left Notes*, October 7, 1966, p. 3
7) Mills, C. Wright: *Power, Politics and People*, p. 368
8) Conant, James: *Slums and Suburbs*, p. 77
9) Rickover, Hyman: *Education and Freedom*, p. 145
10) Conant, James: *Slums and Suburbs*, p. 34
11) Smith, Mortimer: *The Diminished Mind*, p. 87
12) Hannah, John: Speech given at Parents' Convocation at Michigan State University, September, 1961
13) Hannah, John: "The Schools' Responsibility in National Defense," May 5, 1955, quoted in *The Paper*, November 17, 1966, p. 1
14) Conant, James: Bulletin of the Council for Basic Education, Jan. 1960, p. 3
15) Kerr, Clark: *Uses of the University*, p. 87
16) Gorz, Andre: "Capitalism and the Labor Force," *International Socialist Journal*, p. 423   17) Ibid., p. 428   18) Ibid., p. 428
19) Friedenberg, Edgar Z.: *The Nation*, September 20, 1965, p. 72   20) Ibid.
21) Kerr, Clark: "Industrialism and Industrial Man," quoted in "The Mind of Clark," in Draper, Hal (ed.): *Berkeley: The New Student Revolt*, p. 211
22) Ibid.
23) Hoare, Quintin: "Education: Programs and Men," *New Left Review* No. 32, pp. 50-51
24) Kerr, Clark: *Uses of the University*, p. 90   25) Ibid., p. 86
26) Beck, H.P.: Quoted in Aptheker, Bettina: *Big Business and the American University*, p. 7
27) "The Innovation Industry," *Monthly Review*, July-August, 1959
28) Jencks, Christopher: "The Future of American Education," *The Radical Papers*, p. 271
29) Mills, C. Wright: *The Sociological Imagination*, p. 117
30) Mills, C. Wright: *Power, Politics and People*, p. 417
31) Kerr, Clark: *Uses of the University*   32) Ibid., p. 53
33) Gorz, Andre: "Capitalism and the Labor Force," *International Socialist Journal*, p. 417
34) Kerr, Clark: *Uses of the University*, pp. 89-90
35) Gorz, Andre: "Capitalism and the Labor Force," *International Socialist Journal*, p. 418
36) Jencks, Christopher: "The Future of American Education," *The Radical Papers*
37) Kerr, Clark: *Uses of the University*, p. 111
38) Gorz, Andre: *Strategy for Labor*, p. 108
39) Gorz, Andre: "Capitalism and the Labor Force," *International Socialist Journal*, p. 422
40) Gorz, Andre: *Strategy for Labor*, p. 107
41) Guevara, Ernest "Che": *Guerrilla Warfare*
42) Mills, C. Wright: *Power, Politics and People*, p. 386

Published as an SDS pamphlet in the summer of 1967.

TOWARD A
STUDENT SYNDICALIST MOVEMENT, OR
UNIVERSITY REFORM REVISITED

In the past few years, we have seen a variety of campus movements developing around the issue of "university reform." A few of these movements sustained a mass base for brief periods. Some brought about minor changes in campus rules and regulations. But almost all have failed to alter the university community radically or even to maintain their own existence. What is the meaning of this phenomenon? How can we avoid it in the future? Why bother with university reform at all?

It is a belief among members of Students for a Democratic Society that all the issues are interrelated. However, we often fail to relate them in any systematic way. What, in fact, is the connection between dorm hours and the war in Vietnam? Is there one system responsible for both? If so, what is the nature of that system? And, finally, how should we respond? These are the questions I will try to answer in the following analysis.

Why university reform?

SDS has named the existing system in this country "corporate liberalism." And, if we bother to look, its penetration into the campus community is awesome. Its elite is trained in our colleges of business administration. Its defenders are trained in our law schools. Its apologists can be found in the political science departments. The colleges of social sciences produce its manipulators. For propagandists, it relies on the school of journalism. It insures its own future growth in the colleges of education. If some of us don't quite fit in, we are brainwashed in the divisions of counseling. And we all know only too well what goes on in the classrooms of the military science building.

This situation takes on more sinister ramifications when we realize that all these functionaries of "private enterprise" are being trained at the people's expense. American corporations have little trouble increasing the worker's wage, especially when they can take it back in the form of school taxes and tuition to train their future workers. To be sure, many corporations give the universities scholarships and grants. But this is almost always for some purpose of their own, if only for a tax dodge.

Furthermore, the corporate presence on campus grotesquely transforms the nature of the university community. The most overt example is the grade system. Most professors would agree that grades are meaningless, if not positively harmful, to the learning process. But the entire manipulated community replies in unison: "But how else would companies know whom to hire (or the Selective Service whom to draft)?" And we merrily continue to spend public money subsidizing testing enterprises for private enterprise.

What we must see clearly is the relation between the university and corporate liberal society at large. Most of us are outraged when our university administrators or their student government lackeys liken our universities and colleges to corporations. We bitterly respond with talk about a "community of scholars." However, the fact of the matter is that they are correct. Our educational institutions *are* corporations and knowledge factories. What we have failed to see in the past is how absolutely vital these factories are to the corporate liberal state.

What do these factories produce? What are their commodities? The most obvious answer is "knowledge." Our factories produce the know-how that enables the corporate state to expand, to grow, and to exploit people more efficiently and extensively both in our own country and in the third world. But knowledge is perhaps too abstract to be viewed as a commodity. Concretely, the commodities of our factories are the *knowledgeable*. AID [Agency for International Development] officials, Peace Corpsmen, military officers, CIA officials, segregationist judges, corporation lawyers, politicians of all sorts, welfare workers, managers of industry, labor bureaucrats (I could go on and on): Where do they come from? They are products of the factories we live and work in.

It is on our assembly lines in the universities that they are molded into what they are. As integral parts of the knowledge factory system, we are both the exploiters and the exploited. As both the managers and the managed, we produce and become the most vital product of corporate liberalism: bureaucratic man. In short, we are a new kind of scab.

But let us return to our original question. What is the connec-

43

tion between dorm rules and the war in Vietnam? Superficially, both are aspects of corporate liberalism, a dehumanized and oppressive system. But let us be more specific. Who are the dehumanizers and oppressors? In a word, our past, present and future alumni: the finished product of our knowledge factories.

How did they become what they are? They were shaped on an assembly line that starts with children entering junior high school and ends with junior bureaucrats in commencement robes. And the rules and regulations of *in loco parentis* are essential tools along that entire assembly line. Without them, it would be difficult to produce the kind of men that can create, sustain, tolerate, or ignore situations like Watts, Mississippi and Vietnam.

Finally, perhaps we can see the vital connections that our factories have with the present conditions of corporate liberalism when we ask ourselves what would happen if the military found itself without ROTC students, the CIA found itself without recruits, paternalistic welfare departments found themselves without social workers, or the Democratic Party found itself without young liberal apologists and campaign workers? In short, what would happen to a manipulative society if its means of creating *manipulable* people were done away with?

The answer is that we might then have a fighting chance to change that system. Most of us have been involved in university reform movements of one sort or another. For the most part, our efforts have produced very little. The Free Speech Movement flared briefly, then died out. There have been a few dozen *ad hoc* committees for the abolition of this or that rule. Some of these succeed, then fall apart. Some never get off the ground.

However, we have had some effect. The discontent is there. Although the apathy is extensive and deep-rooted, even the apathetic gripe at times. Our administrators are worried. They watch us carefully, have staff seminars on Paul Goodman, and study our own literature more carefully than we do. They handle our outbursts with kid gloves, trying their best not to give us an issue.

We have one more factor in our favor: We have made many mistakes that we can learn from. I will try to enumerate and analyze a few of them.

1) *Forming single-issue groups.* A primary example here is organizing a committee to abolish dorm hours for women students

over 21. This tactic has two faults. First, insofar as relevance is concerned, this is a *felt* issue for less than 10 per cent of the average campus. Hence, it is almost impossible to mobilize large numbers of students around the issue for any length of time. The same criticism applies to student labor unions (only a few hundred students work for the university), dress regulations (only the hippies are bothered), or discrimination in off-campus housing (most black college students are too bourgeois to care). The second fault is that most of these issues can be accommodated by the administration: After months of meetings, speeches and agitation, the dean of women changes the rules so that a woman over 21, with parental permission and a high enough grade average, can apply, if she wants, for a key to the dorm. Big deal. At this stage, the tiny organization that worked for this issue usually folds up.

2) *Organizing around empty issues.* Students often try to abolish rules that aren't enforced anyway. Almost every school has a rule forbidding women to visit men's apartments. But it is rarely enforced, even if openly violated. Since most students are not restricted by the rule, they usually won't fight to change it. Often, they will react negatively, feeling that if the issue is brought up, the administration will have to enforce it.

3) *Fear of being radical.* Time and time again, we water down our demands and compromise ourselves *before we even begin.* In our meetings we argue the administration's position against us before they do and better than they will. We allow ourselves to be intimidated by the word "responsible." (How many times have we changed a "Student Bill of Rights" to a watered-down "Resolution on Student Rights and Responsibilities"?) We spend more energy assuring our deans that we "don't want another Berkeley" than we do talking with students about the real issues.

4) *Working through existing channels.* This phrase really means, "Let us stall you off until the end of the year." If we listen to it at all, we ought to do so just once and in such a way as to show everyone that it's a waste of time.

5) *Waiting for faculty support.* This is like asking Southern Negroes to wait for white moderates. We often failed to realize that the faculty are more powerless than we: They have the welfare of their families to consider.

45

6) *Legal questions.* We spend hours debating among ourselves whether the university can legally abolish *in loco parentis.* They can if they want to, or if they have to. Besides, suppose it isn't legal. Should we then stop, pick up our marbles, and go home?

7) *Isolating ourselves.* Time and time again we fall into the trap of trying to organize independents over the "Greek-Independent split." This should be viewed as an administration plot to divide and rule. On the other hand, we shouldn't waste time trying to court the Greeks or "campus leaders." They haven't any more real power than anyone else. Also, SDS people often view themselves as intellectual enclaves on campus when they should see themselves as organizing committees for the entire campus. We retreat to our own "hippie hangouts" rather than spending time in the student union building talking with others.

8) *Forming Free Universities* This action can be a good thing, depending on how it is organized. But we run the risk of the utopian socialists who withdrew from the early labor struggles. We may feel liberated in our Free Universities; but, in the meantime, the "unfree" university we left goes cranking out corporate liberals. In fact, they have it easier since we aren't around making trouble.

9) *Working within student government.* We should do this for one and only one reason: to abolish the student government. We should have learned by now that student governments have no power and, in many cases, the administration has organized them in such a way that it is impossible to use them to get power. (In a few cases, it might be possible to take over a student government and threaten to abolish it if power isn't granted.)

From these criticisms of our mistakes over the past few years, I think the direction we should move in becomes more clear. Also, when we consider the fact that *our universities are already chief agents for social change in the direction of 1984,* I think we can see why it is imperative that we organize the campuses. (I do not mean to imply that we ought to ignore organizing elsewhere.)

Toward student syndicalism

In the preceding analysis of the university (by no means original with me), we can find an implicit antagonism, or, if you will, a fundamental contradiction. Namely, our administrators ask of us that we both participate and not participate in our educational system. We are told we must learn to make responsible decisions, yet we are not allowed to make actual decisions. We are told that education is an active process, yet we are passively trained. We are criticized for our apathy and for our activism. In the name of freedom, we are trained to obey.

The system requires that we passively agree to be manipulated. But our vision is one of active participation. And this is a demand that our administrators cannot meet without putting themselves out of a job. That is exactly why we should be making the demand.

What is to be done?

Obviously, we need to organize, to build on the campuses a movement that has the primary purpose of radically transforming the university community. Too often we lose sight of this goal. To every program, every action, every position, and every demand, we must raise the question: How will this radically alter the lives of every student on this campus? With this in mind, I offer the following proposals for action.

1) That every SDS chapter organize a student syndicalist movement on its campus. I use the term "syndicalist" for a crucial reason. In the labor struggle, the syndicalist unions worked for industrial democracy and workers' control, rather than for better wages and working conditions. Similarly, and I cannot repeat this often enough, the issue for us is student control (along with a yet-to-be liberated faculty in some areas). What we do not want is a company-union type of student movement that sees itself as a body that, under the rubric of "liberalization," helps a paternal administration make better rules for us. What we do want is a union of students in which the students themselves decide what kind of rules they want or don't want. Or whether they need rules at all. Only this sort of student organization allows for decentralization and the direct participation of students in all those decisions daily affecting their lives.

2) That the student syndicalist movement take on one of two possible structures: a Campus Freedom Democratic Party (CFDP) or a Free Student Union (FSU).

47

a) *Campus Freedom Democratic Party.* This is possible on those campuses where the existing student government is at least formally democratic (that is, one student—one vote). The idea is to organize a year-round electoral campaign for the purposes of educating students about their system; building mass memberships in dormitory and living-area "precincts"; constantly harassing and disrupting the meetings of the existing student government (for instance, showing up *en masse* at at a meeting and singing the jingle of the now-defunct "Mickey Mouse Club"); and, finally, winning a majority of seats in student government elections. As long as the CFDP has a minority of seats, those seats should be used as soapboxes to expose the existing body as a parody of the idea of government. It should be kept in mind that the main purpose of these activities is to develop a radical consciousness among *all* the students in the struggle yet to come against the administration.

What happens if a CFDP wins a majority of the seats? It should immediately push through a list of demands (the nature of which I will deal with later) in the form of a Bill of Rights or Declaration of Independence or both. The resolution should indicate a time-limit for the administration (or regents or whatever) to reply. If the demands are met, the students should promptly celebrate the victory of the revolution. If not, the CFDP should promptly abolish student government or set up a student-government-in-exile. Second, the CFDP should immediately begin mass demonstrations: sit-ins in the administration buildings, in faculty parking-lots, in maintenance departments, and so forth; boycotts of all classes; and strikes of teaching assistants. In short, the success of these actions (especially when the cops come) will be the test of how well the CFDP has been radicalizing its constituency during the previous two or three years.

b) *Free Student Union.* The difference between an FSU and a CFDP is mainly tactical. On many campuses, existing student governments are not even formally democratic; rather, they are set up with the school newspaper having one vote, the interfraternity council having one vote, and so on. In a situation like this, we ought to ignore or denounce campus or electoral politics from the word go, and, following the plan of the Wobblies, organize one big union of all students. The first goal of the FSU would be to develop a counter-institution to the existing student government that would eventually embrace a healthy majority of the student body. It would have to encourage non-participation in student government and to engage in active, non-electoral, "on-the-job" agitation. This would take the form of organizing and sponsoring the violation of existing rules. Such violations might include staging dormitory sleep-outs and "freedom" parties in restricted apartments, nonviolently seizing the building that houses IBM machines used to grade tests, campaigning to mutilate IBM cards, disrupting oversized classes, and nonviolently attempting to occupy and liberate the student newspaper and radio station. All this should be done in such a manner as to recruit more and more support. Once the FSU has more support than the student government has, it should declare the student government defunct, make its demands of the administration, and, if refused, declare the general strike.

Obviously, the success of either a CFDP or an FSU depends upon our ability to organize a mass radical base with a capacity for prolonged resistance, dedication and endurance. Bearing these needs in mind, one can easily see why such a student syndicalist movement must be national (or even international) in its scope. There will be a need for highly mobile regional and national full-time organizers to travel from campus to campus. When critical confrontations break out, there will be a need for sympathy demonstrations and strikes on other campuses. There may even be a need to send busloads of students to a campus where, because of mass arrests, replacements are required. Again, we can learn much from the organizing tactics of the Wobblies and the CIO.

3) That the student syndicalist movement adopt as its primary and central issue *the abolition of the grade system*. This is not to say that other issues, such as decision-making power for student government bodies, are unimportant. They are not; and, in certain situations, they can be critical. But to my mind, the abolition of grades is the most significant over-all issue for building a radical movement on campus. There are three reasons why I think this is so:

a) Grading is a *common condition* of the total student and faculty community. It is the direct cause of most student anxieties and frustrations. Also, it is the cause of the alienation of most faculty members from their work. Among our better educators and almost all faculty, there is a consensus that grades are, at best, meaningless, and more likely, harmful to real education.

b) As an issue to organize around, the presence of the grade system is *constantly felt*. Hour exams, midterms and finals are always cropping up (whereas student government elections occur only once a year). Every time we see our fellow students cramming for exams (actually, for grades), we can point out to them that they are being exploited and try to organize them. In every class we take, throughout the school year, every time our professors grade our papers and tests, we can agitate in our classrooms, exposing the system and encouraging both our classmates and our instructors to join with us to abolish that system.

c) The abolition of the grade system is a demand that cannot be met by the administration without radically altering the shape and purpose of our educational system. First of all, if there were no grades, a significant part of our administrators would be without jobs, for they would have nothing to do. Also, large mass-production TV classes and the like would have to be done away with. Since education would have to take place through personal contact between the student and his professor, classes would necessarily be limited in size. Since the evaluation of a student's work would not have to be temporally regulated and standardized, independent scholarship would be encouraged, if not necessitated. As a result, the corporate might have some difficulty in finding manipulable junior bureaucrats. Finally, the Selective Service would have a hell of a time ranking us.

For these reasons, it is my feeling that the abolition of the grade system should serve as the "umbrella" issue for a student syndicalist movement, much in the same manner as the abolition of the wage system served the syndicalist trade union movement. Under this umbrella, many other issues can be raised, depending upon which segment of the student community we were appealing to and upon what degree of strength we might have at any one time.

4) That the student syndicalist movement incorporate in secondary issues the ideology of participatory democracy. This can be viewed as an attempt on our part to sabotage the knowledge factory machinery that produces the managers and the managed of 1984. There are numerous ways to go about this. I will list a few:

a) Approach students in teachers' colleges with a counter-curriculum that is based on the ideas of Paul Goodman and A. S. Neill for the radical education of children.

b) At the beginning of each semester, request (or demand) of the professors that you and your fellow classmates participate in shaping the structure, format and content of that particular course.

c) Sign up for, attend, denounce, and then walk out of and picket excessively large classes.

d) Organize students and liberated faculty members in certain departments to work out a model counter-curriculum and agitate for its adoption, *mainly because students participated in shaping it* rather than because of its merits.

e) Hold mock trials for the dean of men and dean of women for their "crimes against humanity."

f) In the case of women students, organize a decentralized federation of dormitory councils (soviets?) where each living unit would formulate a counter-set of rules and regulations; and then use them to replace existing rules *on the grounds that the women themselves made the rules.*

I am sure that if we use our imaginations, we can extend this list indefinitely. And because they embody the philosophy of participatory democracy, these suggestions, to my mind, are of intrinsic worth. And I also believe that they might have far-reaching effects. For participatory democracy is often like a chronic and contagious disease. Once caught, it permeates one's whole life and the lives of those around. Its effect is disruptive in a total sense. And within a manipulative, bureaucratic system, its articulation and expression amounts to sabotage. It is my hope that those exposed to it during the time they are building a movement for student syndicalism will never quite be the same, especially after they leave the university community.

Position paper delivered at the August 1966 SDS Convention

TOWARD INSTITUTIONAL RESISTANCE

The recent confrontations on our campuses between radical students and recruiters from the military and the war industries demonstrate the beginnings of a new phase of struggle within the anti-war movement. The resistance being offered campus officials and civil police by radical students is almost without precedent in the history of the American university. As radicals, we unequivocally celebrate the recent events at the Universities of Wisconsin and Illinois, and at Brooklyn and Oberlin Colleges. But celebration is not enough. We must critically evaluate the present conflicts in order to draw lessons for the future.

The current battles are not without a history, however young the movement might seem. The first student protests against the Vietnam war go back to 1963. Beginning in the fall of 1964, the teach-in movement swept across American campuses for almost two years. Hundreds of thousands in the academic community turned against the government's policy in Southeast Asia. On almost every campus a dissident and active minority took root and grew. After an initial showing of 25,000 at the SDS April 17, 1965 March on Washington, a primarily campus-based anti-war movement turned out over 200,000 demonstrators in nearly 150 cities for the fall 1965 International Days of Protest.

Before the Spring of 1966, the campus was seen primarily as a haven and recruiting ground for the anti-war movement, with periodic public demonstrations and teach-ins continuing to be our principal tactics. During this period there were only a handful of sporadic leafletings and picketings of CIA and Marine Corps recruiters on campus. The issue of university complicity with the war was not raised until April and May of 1966. During that time, shortly after major escalations of the war, the student movement had been developing a program of opposition to the draft. Concurrently, the Selective Service System initiated requirements for the ranking of male students by their grade averages and scores on a National SSS exam, to be given on 1200 campuses in May

1966. SDS attacked the exam, the draft, 2S deferments, the war, and, most importantly, university complicity with the war by ranking male students and holding the Selective Service exams. Demonstrations again swept the campuses. Thousands of students sat-in and hundreds were arrested at the University of Chicago, Roosevelt, Buffalo, Brooklyn College, University of Wisconsin, Cornell, Stanford and CCNY. The government eventually abolished class rank and the tests, probably as a result of the sit-ins and the threat of more to come.

However, the issue of university complicity with the war remained in the consciousness of the student movement. Already alienated from college administrations as a result of the free-speech and *in loco parentis* fights of 1964 and 1965, the radical student movement began a deeper probe of the university's connections with the military. In the winter of 1966 the University of Pennsylvania students gained nationwide publicity for uncovering chemical and bacteriological war research for Vietnam on their campus. *Ramparts* magazine had already exposed Michigan State University's cooperation with the CIA in developing Diem's police state. Several SDS chapters had picketed and protested against military recruiters on campus. The first major confrontation occurred at Berkeley, early in December of 1966. SDS members on the campus attempted to set up an anti-draft table next to a Navy recruiting table in the student union. The administration called in the police and a massive sit-in began. To break the sit-in, over 100 police were used. Nine students were arrested and scores were injured. Over 10,000 students rallied and formulated the demands for a strike. Five days later, the strike was broken, though it had been 70% effective in the first two days.

While the students might have lost the battle of Berkeley, the event sparked the beginning of a series of similar conflicts across the country. From January to June, for the remainder of the school year, demonstrations and sit-ins against the presence on campus of recruiters from the military and related institutions were commonplace. Columbia University, Iowa State and the University of Wisconsin saw major sit-ins against CIA recruiters. Beginning in January at Brown University, recruiters from Dow Chemical Company, manufacturers of napalm, were confronted on several dozen campuses. Major anti-Dow sit-ins occurred at the University of Wisconsin, San Fernando Valley State, UCLA and Claremont College. At Claremont, students not only drove the Dow recruiter off campus, but literally chased him out of town. In April 1967, Columbia University SDS organized a massive and significant confrontation with Marine recruiters, with 800 students almost physically removing the Marines from campus, while fighting off violent attacks from a smaller group of 200 right-wing students.

Finally, during the two days before the Spring Mobilization, SDS at the New School for Social Research organized an 80% effective strike against the war. While the New School Strike was a symbolic action without any specific demands of the college administration, it was an important event, indicating to the student movement that student strikes were a viable strategy.

The most interesting aspect of the scores of similar confrontations between radical students and recruiters from Dow, the CIA and the military is that the events were unplanned an unconnected on the national level. Furthermore, they received relatively little coverage in the national news media. It seems that SDS's weekly newspaper, *New Left Notes*, deserves most of the credit for spreading the actions, since it covered the first actions against Dow and the military in detail. SDS chapters probably picked up on the strategy from there, and followed with similar actions on their local campuses. While the SDS national staff certainly approved of and encouraged the confrontations, the major part of its time and resources during that period were spent developing a draft resistance program and organizing regional educational conferences. The idea of organizing a national movement to expel the military from the campus was never suggested as an SDS national program until late March of 1967 in an article in *New Left Notes* by Todd Gitlin. The strategy formally became a major SDS national program at the June 1967 National Convention in Ann Arbor, Michigan.

In the time between the confrontations ending with spring semester of 1967 and the present struggles this fall, the radical student movement has gone through several significant changes. To better understand both the actions of our past activities as well as the direction of our present and future struggles on the campus, we must consider those developments.

First of all, we have grown. The Vietnam war continues filling our ranks with fresh recruits. Not only has the left grown, but all sectors of the population have become increasingly dissatisfied with the war, especially the campus community. In addition to building our numerical strength, the war has constantly and consistently pushed us to the left politically, strategically and tactically. Who among us today would argue that America is not an imperialist power? Less than a year ago, only the "crazy left sectarians" used that language. Now even clergymen talk about imperialism. Draft resistance activity is commonplace. Less than two years ago, SDS went through a major political crisis over simply printing a *proposal* for anti-draft activity. We no longer talk about moving from protest to resistance. The resistance has already begun.

Apart from the war, the black ghetto rebellions this summer fundamentally altered the political reality of white America, including the white left. The black liberation movement has replaced the civil rights and anti-poverty movements, revealing the utter bankruptcy of corporate liberalism's co-optive programs. The events of this summer marked not only the possibility, but the beginning of the second American revolution. This second factor has made more important than ever the organizing of white poor and workingclass communities by the white radicals. SDS is beginning a response to this situation which includes a major refocusing of draft resistance work away from the student community and into poor and workingclass communities.

Thirdly, in the past few months, SDS people have had to deal with an increasing repression, often violent, from the state and its supporters. Some of us have fared better than others, but no one goes limp anymore, or meekly to jail. Police violence does not go unanswered. Sit-ins are no longer symbolic, but strategic: to protect people or hold positions, rather than to allow oneself to be passively stepped over or carted off. The implications of this change, asserting itself for the first time nationally on the Pentagon steps October 21st, are more important than one might assume. For instance, while the anti-recruiting sit-ins last spring were primarily acts of moral witness and political protest, an increasing number of the sit-ins this fall displayed the quality of tactical political resistance. Their purpose was the disruption and obstruction of certain events and actions *by whatever means necessary*. Politically, the occurrence of this kind of activity implies the prior dissolution of whatever legitimacy and authority the institutions being resisted may have formerly had. This exceedingly important process of desanctification points to the weakening of the existing institutions of power as well as the growing revolutionary potential of those forces opposing that power.

The final factor we should take into account has been the development over the past six months of an analysis and strategy for institutional resistance. Near the end of 1966, SDS emerged from a dormant and disconnected summer with a mood and rhetoric of resistance. By the beginning of 1967, that rhetoric had little substantive content, except for an audacious but unimplemented draft-resistance program. When the present school year started, we seemed to be somewhat better off. We had an analysis and strategy, at least in part. We had begun the task of developing the politics of anti-imperialism within a growing anti-war movement. We developed an analysis of the university as a "knowledge factory" adjunct to the multinational cororations of American capitalism. Our factories had the task of supplying an expanding but orderly flow of two valuable and strategic commodities into American business, government and military institutions—manpower and intelligence. During the summer, our research into the penetration and use of the university by military and paramilitary operations revealed extensive connections with organizations like Project Themis, IDA, TRICAT, RAND, Project Agile, and CRESS, to name a few.* All of these had, in one way or another, commandeered the work and energy of our schools and had put our resources to the ends of the present and future oppression and domination of the people of the world, both in Vietnam and in our urban ghettoes. We found our own unfreedom in the face of those IBM bureaucracies tied to the oppression of people everywhere.

SDS had always urged powerless people to take power in those institutions affecting their daily lives. We now fully understood the impossibility of freedom in the university so long as it remained tied to the interests of America's corporate and military ruling elite. Secondly, we saw the possibility of engaging in a common struggle with the liberation movements of the world by con-

* Specializing in weapons research or counter-insurgency warfare research projects, these government-funded university-based organizations were the major links between American "higher education" and the U.S. war machine (Publisher's Note).

fronting the on-campus sector of the same military apparatus oppressing them. Our strategy became clear: the disruption, dislocation and destruction of the military's access to the manpower, intelligence or resources of our universities. Our tactics: a varied series of local confrontations with campus military and paramilitary operations hopefully escalating into student strikes, culminating in a national student strike in the spring of 1968 against the military's presence on campus and against the war in Vietnam. This was by no means seen as our only program, even by the campus. But it was to be a major effort and experiment in a strategy of institutional resistance.

Thus far, SDS has confronted a moderate range of military and counterinsurgency operations on campus. The work of these operations falls into three general areas: 1) recruiting, 2) research and development or R & D, and 3) classroom training.

In the area of recruiting, we have confronted, at a variety of levels, the Army, Navy, Marines, Air Force, CIA, Dow Chemical, Peace Corps, Vista and ROTC. Concerning research, we have had little experience, the only major exceptions being the discontinuance of a CBW [Chemical and Bacteriological Warfare] project called "Spicerack" at the University of Pennsylvania and the temporary disruption of IDA offices at Princeton University.

In the classroom, we have disrupted or otherwise rendered temporarily disfunctional a range of ROTC training sessions on several campuses, as well as regular foreign policy courses following the government line. One imaginative confrontation in this area was with a TRICAT (Triennial Civil Affairs Training, Army Reserve) counterinsurgency seminar on Greece at the University of Florida. Several dozen SDS pickets, complete with sound truck, calling themselves the People's Liberation Army made a surprise appearance at the Army's Saturday morning COIN lectures. After surrounding the building, they quickly leafleted the classes, gave short speeches over their PA system, planted an insurgent flag on top of the building and disappeared. Other confrontations involved a major resistance to and defeat of the ranking and testing process of the SSS and several successful occasions of resisting HUAC's overt attempts at gathering campus information on radical students.

The tactics we have developed thus far cover a wide range, beginning with mild dissent and protest, and reaching to forceful resistance. The selection of tactics naturally depends on one's strength relative to a particular opponent within the limits of the current political situation. In general, we have been underestimating our own strength and overestimating the enemy. The following list attempts to present a general outline of the tactics we have used and developed in the last two years of confrontation:

1) individual vocal dissension, questions and speeches at recruiting areas.

2) attending, officially or unofficially, training classes and "teaching-in," either on a one-shot basis or for the duration of the course.

3) leafleting training classes with counter-information, counter-readings, and counter-exams and/or holding counter-classes.

4) leafleting recruiting areas and research sites.

5) exposing secret research and/or exposing clandestine connections of open research, recruiting or training institutes in campus and national news media.

6) making appointments with recruiters in order to debate, harass and/or to take up their time.

7) obtaining favorable resolutions against current and future recruiting, research and/or training from student governments, faculty senates, and other groups.

8) placing "war crimes" and other dramatic posters at recruiting sites or training classrooms.

9) setting up counter tables next to recruiting tables or training classrooms.

10) picketing recruiting areas or training classrooms.

11) staging "guerrilla theater" with death-masks, posters, props and pictures in recruiting areas and training classrooms.

12) holding teach-ins before, during and after recruiting, training or research work.

13) holding "war crimes trials" for recruiters, trainees and researchers.

14) holding a "guerrilla siege" of building(s) during counterinsurgency classes.

15) holding speaking forums, questionings and rallies drawing sufficient numbers into recruiting or training areas in order to indirectly stop or disrupt the recruiting or training process.

16) holding non-obstructive sit-ins at recruiting sites, leaving

a pathway cleared for recruitees.

17) holding obstructive sit-ins at recruiting sites to prevent recruiting:

  a) passive: recruitee or others can pass if they use force.

  b) active: recruitee or others using force to pass will be met with counter-force by those sitting-in.

18) holding obstructive or non-obstructive sit-ins at administration offices to bring pressure for the cancelation of recruiting, training or research.

19) holding obstructive sit-ins around automobiles and/or campus entrances to prevent recruiters and/or police cars or paddy wagons containing arrested students from leaving.

20) tipping over recruiting tables and/or seizing recruiting literature.

21) removing recruiters and/or police from campus by force or threat of force.

22) organizing a student strike until administrators stop the activity of certain recruiters, researchers, training classes, police action, or their own reprisals.

Naturally, this list is not meant to be inclusive of all our tactics, only the most common. Also, there are no set formulas for deciding which tactics to use in any given situation. However, there are a few guidelines to keep in mind. First, and most important, don't become *isolated* by using tactics likely to divide the participants in the action from their present and *potential* constituency. But even our potential constituents are limited, and we shouldn't try to please everyone. The problem is not whether or not one makes enemies, but whether or not one has the right people for enemies.

Secondly, the tactics of the resistance struggle should result in two complementary goals: 1) the weakening of the resisted dominant institution, and 2) developing a consciousness of power among those resisting the dominant institutions. Towards this end, we shouldn't be afraid to proclaim a victory when we're ahead; and then retreating, rather than allowing a resistance struggle to degenerate into a symbolic protest and defeat. A perfect example of this situation was the Pentagon siege on October 21st. The high point and victory of the resistance struggle occurred near dusk, after we had broken military lines, occupied *their territory*, entered the Pentagon, and held our ground until the point where two of their soldiers came over to us. At that point, we should have declared a victory and marched away, rather than sitting there, hour after hour, in slowly weakening and decreasing numbers, waiting for our final symbolic defeat.

A final guideline, a corollary of the first, is that a resistance must grow both in numbers, and in depth of commitment, if it is to survive and eventually win. Most important in this area is political education, for both ourselves and our potential constituency. For example, *we* may know about the CIA, but what about the rest of the campus? And the surrounding academic community? Before we use tactics like obstructive sit-ins, we must be careful to carry out extensive educational work, such as speeches, leaflets, rallies, or teach-ins, both on and off the campus.

My next criticism deals with those anti-military protests on campus that have contained their objections to the work of the war machine within the limits of academic policy. While it is true that, say, secret research is poor academic policy, we are not opposed to it because of its cluttering up academia, but because it is directly a part of the apparatus dominating and oppressing most of the world's people. To limit our opposition to recruiting and research because "they are disruptive of the academic and educational atmosphere" is to enclose ourselves within the elitist ivory tower academias of the past centuries. We are interested in building a movement of ordinary people, rather than one of academics still swayed by such arguments.

A third question, rather than criticism, we have been forced to deal with by recent events is the issue of civil liberties. Objection after objection has been made that by obstructing recruiters, we have been denying others—the recruiter and those who wish to see him—the right of free speech and assembly. In a sense, this is true. As I mentioned earlier, the institutions our resistance has desanctified and delegitimatized, as a result of our action *against the oppression of others*, have lost all authority and, hence, all respect. As such, they have only raw, coercive power. Since they are without legitimacy in our eyes, they are without rights. Insofar as individuals, such as recruiters, continue to remain in association with those institutions, they run the risk of being given the same treatment. Most people agree with this position *in principle*. There are very few who would argue that we should not stop, rather than debate, individuals who might have recruited for the staff needed to operate Hitler's death-camps.

The question we are asked to answer, rather, is by what criteria do we determine whether or not an institution or individual has lost their legitimacy. There are two kinds of answers, one within bourgeois thought, the other without. For the first, we can assert the Nuremburg decisions and other past criteria of war crimes as the criteria by which we, in conscience, decide whether or not an institution and individuals associated with that institution have lost their legitimacy and their rights. Our second answer rests in a revolutionary critique of the institutions and society we are trying to destroy. Our critique argues that the social order we are rebelling against is totalitarian, manipulative, repressive and anti-democratic. Furthermore, within this order of domination, to respect and operate within the realm of bourgeois civil liberties is to remain enslaved, since the legal apparatus is designed to sustain the dominant order, containing potential forces for change within its pre-established and ultimately castrating confines. As a result, it is the duty of a revolutionary not only to be intolerant of, but to actually suppress the anti-democratic activities of the dominant order.

There are other answers as well as these two. One is that the recruiters haven't come to debate, only to recruit; hence free speech is not the issue. Most recruiters will help you out on this one by refusing a public debate. After he refuses, we can make the point that he decided himself that free speech wasn't the issue. No matter what they say, however, we are bound to find much opposition on this issue. Which is often good, since it raises substantive questions that work toward the deobfuscation of the reality of American power.

While it remains an important strategy, institutional resistance to the military presence on campus is not a panacea for revolutionary change in the United States. It is not even a complete strategy for an anti-war movement, but only one facet. However, it seems to contain within it, not only significant lessons and possibilities for the student movement, but also ideas that might be central, to the development of analysis, strategy and tactics for other battlefronts within the American Leviathan as well.

New Left Notes,
November 13, 1967

AFTERWORD

These writings were produced on the road, in the heat of battle, with hardly any looking back with an editor's eye for polishing rough edges. At the time, I never imagined they would have the impact that they did then or the interest they continue to draw today.

They were practical documents. We produced them to fan the flames, to take the lessons learned, good and bad, in one place, and pass them on to the next campus, the next region, and even, eventually, the next country.

Our practice, especially in those early years, was fueled by the New Left's vision of revolutionary democracy. Our consciousness had been transformed by the Black upsurge in the Deep South. We felt firsthand the extraordinary solidarity and spiritual power of ordinary men and women determined to bring down fearful enemies. The experience helped us break with the futile compromises of a tired liberalism, and inspired us to try to work out a new analysis of society and new methods for change.

Toward a Student Syndicalist Movement was a first effort. I wrote it at the University of Nebraska, where I was a graduate student in philosophy, immediately after returning from a march through Mississippi where the "Black Power" slogan had just been launched. Its core insight was that students were not simply catalysts for change in the organizing of other constituencies off the campus, but had become a critical social force in their own right. The task was to organize them for power, and to form alliances with other forces, such as Blacks and workers, also seeking empowerment.

My fellow activists loved the word "Syndicalism" in the title. I put it there deliberately to form a link with an earlier tradition of radical democracy in *American* history, the labor struggles of the Industrial Workers of the World (IWW). Others saw it as a way to tweak the liberalism and Stalinism of the older generation of the left. I mimeographed the paper for use in a workshop at the 1966 SDS national convention in Clear Lake, Iowa. I had no hint that it would fire the imagination of most of the delegates or that I would be elected to national leadership as a result. The paper was later translated and reprinted in dozens of papers, books and journals around the world.

New Radicals in the Multiversity was a more serious effort of linking our practice with a new and deeper analysis of capitalism. I lived on the road, traveling from campus to campus, as I researched and wrote parts of it. Major sections were written in the loft of a rock'n'roll club in Los Angeles, in a Chicago skid row restaurant named Vic West's, and in the West End Cafe near Columbia University in New York.

During this period I was part of the "Praxis Axis," a loose group-

62

ing in SDS that tried to use the work of Herbert Marcuse and the French neo-Marxists, Serge Mallet and Andre Gorz, to work through a new analysis of the university and society. It included Greg Calvert, Bob Gottlieb, Naomi Jaffe, Dave Gilbert and others. In particular, we expanded on Mallet's idea of "the new working class," referring to that new sector of the economy where most students would go after gradiation. We were fascinated with the potential of the "information revolution" just getting under way, but we also stressed its negative side. We introduced the term "underclass" to designate those suffering from near-permanent structural unemployment.

But this fledgling effort at revolutionary theorizing was swept away by the profound events of the year 1968. The assassinations of Martin Luther King and Bobby Kennedy, and the dramatic escalation of the war in Vietnam, turned the campuses and inner-city streets into battlegrounds. Stopping the war machine and the racist assault on Black America became the main task, so our analytical work was shifted to disrupting and breaking all university connections with the war effort.

This was the setting for *Toward Institutional Resistance*, which I pulled together after a hurried tour of dozens of campus confrontations and major strikes. My goal was to showcase the history of tactics in some of the more advanced battles so students in less developed situations could learn from them without being intimidated by the militancy. Half seriously, half jokingly, we called it a manual on how to go from passing out leaflets to shutting down the campus in twenty-five steps.

The enemy wasn't amused. One day I found it reprinted in *The Congressional Record* with speeches by hard-right Congressmen denouncing it. As a result, I later learned, the Senate Internal Security Subcommittee put me on a list, circulated to university officials, of 100 people who should not be allowed on campus to speak. Naturally, students wanted to get their hands on the list to find out who to invite. Next I found the article reprinted by the Soviet bloc's International Union of Students, and it traveled on from there to other countries and publications.

I hope student activists today will read these works with a critical outlook. There is a lot in them that still holds true, but much is limited by time, place and circumstance. We were at our best when we based ourselves in the reality of the time and used fresh tools to make sense of it; we were at our worst when we mechanically copied lessons from other periods and situations. Finally, try to read them by mixing the deadly serious character of the events with a small spark of humor and joy in life. That's also the spirit in which they were written.

Carl Davidson

Chicago, September 1990